U-TURN
in the
Single Lane

A Single Woman's Guide
for Overcoming Obstacles, Finding Healing, and Celebrating Purpose

Amy Rae Butler

Carpenter's Son Publishing

U-Turn in the Single Lane

©2016 by Amy Rae Butler

Published by Carpenter's Son Publishing, Franklin, Tennessee

Published in association with Larry Carpenter of Christian Book Services, LLC of Franklin, Tennessee

Edited by Alice Sullivan

Cover and Interior Design by Suzanne Lawing

ISBN: 978-1-942587-46-0

Printed in the United States of America

Contents

Acknowledgments

With special thanks:

To my mother for being an amazing role model in my life and supporting me and encouraging me through all of the trials and heartaches I went through. I do not know where I would be today without your amazing and self-sacrificing love. Thank you for always being there for me. **To my husband** for being such an amazing encourager and support. You were the happy ending to my story. Thank you for challenging me to be a better person. I look forward to the destiny God is going to walk us into. **To Nathan and Anna**, my children—you teach me every day to appreciate the small things and continually remind me that I am so blessed to be a mom.

To Michelle Moore for being such an amazing friend, mentor, and inspiration. Your obedience to God to start a writing class at our church planted a seed in me that God has grown into a ministry. Thank you for all the times you were there for me while I pursued a purpose God called me to.

To Pastors Danny and Jill Chambers for being amazing pastors of Oasis Church and for pouring your life into ministry. Sitting under your leadership and sermons taught me how to grow in the Lord like never before.

To my editor, Alice Sullivan, who has blessed me with not only her editing skills but also her friendship. Your encouragement along the way has been a blessing.

To Larry Carpenter of Clovercroft Publishing for guiding me through the publishing process, always offering advice, and answering my many questions. You made publishing a great experience. **To Steve and Tawnya Sawdy**, who made publishing possible.

Introduction

To all the single women...

So we are single. So what! We should all salute the single woman.

She is *brave* for walking alone in this world.

She is *bold* for being the sole leader of her destiny.

She is *wise* for making her own choices.

She is *strong* for waking up every day and facing the responsibilities of life on her own.

She has *guts* to pull her comforter over her head night after night with no one beside her.

She is *admirable* for finding an identity in herself and not in the efforts of another.

She is *determined* because she puts on the cloak of perseverance every day.

> *For God did not give us a spirit of cowardice, but rather*
> *a spirit of power and of love and of self-discipline.*
> (2 TIMOTHY 1:7 NRSV)

I started writing this book in 2013 when I was single and had finally learned to stop a cycle I had been in for twelve years. I made a bad decision in my early adult years that broke my spirit, got my life off track, and sent me speeding down a road of one disappointment after another in the area of love and dating.

At the age of twenty-four, just a short time after I had graduated from a Christian university, my Cinderella dream was shattered, and I encountered a traumatic situation that left internal emotional scars that altered who I was. Instead of taking time to heal, I became stuck in a cycle of making bad choices in men, using each relationship to mask the wounds I never dealt with.

Some may call it codependent or desperate, but I see it now as a lack of accepting my independence. I was uncomfortable and lonely by myself, so instead of facing my fears, I drove down a road called "Searching for a man to fill the void."

I didn't know at the beginning that I was making bad choices; I seemed to date men who appeared to be really good packages on the outside. But after walking through many years of heartache, I ended up in a place I never dreamed that I would be—as a single mom raising two small children. One would think that I would have taken a long hiatus from men, period, considering the traumatic relationships I had experienced, but I still tried to be in the driver's seat of my own life, and I kept driving from one void filler to another. I kept hoping and searching for a true soul mate kind of love that I had always longed for. I wanted a godly man with outstanding character, but it seemed there was none available; or maybe who I was at that point in life was not able to attract that kind of man.

I wanted things in my time instead of waiting on God's timing. I ran from being alone and facing the true inner healing and self-discovery that I needed. And I ran right into the World Wide Web to find love.

On the outside I appeared to have it all together: a master's degree, my own home, a stable teaching career, a church where I was an active member, and great children. But on the inside, I wasn't sure of who I was, and I certainly did not know how to find wholeness in Christ. Day after day, I was watching the dating websites and hoping I'd have mail in my inbox. Finally, after a few years of relationship disappointments from Internet beaus and men not panning out to be who they said they were, I'd had enough.

Why was I running from being single? Why was I hoping to find someone to love my kids and me and end my hardships as a single mom? A man could not rescue me! I had a void that I had not yet learned to fill with the right thing. I had never taken time to truly discover who I was as a single woman because I was too busy focusing on pleasing someone else and being what someone else needed—this applied not only to men but also to my children.

One night I found myself in tears while kneeling at the end of my bed. I had reached the end of my rope, or rather the end of my own ways. I was weary of sifting through men and tired of going through one short-term dating relationship after another. I didn't want to run from being single anymore. I wanted to embrace it and learn how to be fulfilled by my Maker, my heavenly Husband. I wanted to be strong in Christ and content in Him and who I am. So I made up my mind that I would find a life of fulfillment as a single mom no matter how long it took for God to bring someone into my life, if He ever did. I no longer wanted to run ahead of God's plan for me.

I began to trust Him more than ever, that He was ordering my steps in all aspects of my life as long as I sought Him. There is nothing wrong with being single, and when I learned to view my status differently, I began to see it as a valuable season of life.

So at the age of thirty-six, I made a U-turn in my single life. I turned from trying to find love my way and in my time onto a path of seeking Jesus with reckless abandon. I faced my deeply buried wounds and learned to forgive those who hurt me as well as forgive myself. I learned what it meant to be whole in Christ, and I sought Him more than ever to become whole. I died to all expectations of ever having anyone in my life, and I became content in being just me.

And I can honestly say that that year and a half of my life, of feeling like I was living a fabulous and fulfilling single life in Christ, was the most fulfilling time I had ever experienced. I certainly never dreamed God would have a surprise for me so soon.

As I was writing this book (walking in purpose by using a talent He has given me), to my surprise, God greatly blessed me and brought across my path the kind of man I had always longed for. I wasn't looking for him, for once, and this wonderful man was not found as a result of my searching. God ordained both of our paths to cross.

Toward the end of our first year of marriage, God kept telling me to finish the book and fulfill a vision I had established for my life when I was single. Although I am married now, I still have the desire to share my trials and triumphs with single women who also struggle with one disappointment after another in their dating lives. If I can help one woman choose the road that leads to fulfillment in Christ, versus a road that leads to a torn-up life with many scars because she settled, then my journey of trials and victories has been worth it all.

Single woman, you are amazing, and there is an unbelievable life waiting to be embraced, whether you choose to marry or not. The journey of a single woman is not always easy because it forces you to face yourself and move beyond your comfort zone. Being single is not a life status umbrella that you should hide under while you wait for your dreams to come true. Being single is an awesome time to carpe diem! Seize the moments! Seize the days! And seize every opportunity you can to make this the best season of your life.

If you do desire to marry and be an awesome wife and perhaps even a mother, your single years are the best time to prepare yourself for partnership as you strive to become the kind of woman you want to be. It is an amazing time of growth if you choose to see it that way.

Life is what we *choose* to make it. Choose to make your single life one of the most valuable times of your entire life!

Section One:
Rising from the Ashes

Do not rejoice over me, my enemy; when I fall, I will arise;
when I sit in darkness, the LORD will be a light to me.
(MICAH 7:8 NKJV)

"and provide for those who grieve in Zion—to bestow on them a
crown of beauty instead of ashes, the oil of joy instead of mourn-
ing, and a garment of praise instead of a spirit of despair. They
will be called oaks of righteousness, a planting of the Lord for the
display of his splendor."
(ISAIAH 61:3 NIV)

1

A Second Chance at Life

The LORD is near to all who call on him,
to all who call on him in truth.
He fulfills the desires of those who fear him;
he hears their cry and saves them.
(PSALM 145:18–19 NIV)

Women who stay in unhealthy relationships can often create unhealthy lives for not only themselves but also their children. Children often repeat the pattern they witness growing up. Looking back, perhaps my willingness to settle for unhealthy relationships became acceptable for me due to what I witnessed growing up. Could it be that my relationship issues stemmed from a seed planted in me at a young age? It is very likely.

My father is a wonderful man in many ways, but in his younger years he had issues that stemmed from his own abusive childhood that he had not healed from, and he was repeating the cycle. As a young girl, I saw my father hit my brother on several occasions in anger, and I knew that some nights, when my brother and I were asleep, my mother became the object of his wrath. At nine and a half years old, I witnessed my father trying to wrap a coat hanger around her neck, and amid frantic screams, I shoved him away from my mom. She knew at that moment, something had to change. The next day we packed our bags for a time-out period and left to visit family in Florida. That road trip to Florida marked the true beginning of my story.

THE MAN IN WHITE

On the way back from Florida, on June 24, 1984, our car radiator overheated on Interstate 26. We pulled to the side of the road and waited for help to come. This was long before many people had cell phones, so all we could do was sit and wait for someone to stop to help. My mom was still in the driver's seat, and my brother had just opened the passenger door and was about to attempt to hook up a CB radio when he saw the car heading toward us. When he realized the man was not going to stop, he ran as fast as he could out of the way. My mom and I had no time to react.

A man had fallen asleep at the wheel and hit our parked car at sixty-five miles an hour. My mom was thrown into the passenger side of the car, but by the grace of God she was not thrown out of the door my brother had left open. The shattered windshield left glass embedded in her head and arms.

After the impact, my brother ran to the car in terror. He was able to communicate with my mom, but I was not responsive. He couldn't see me breathing, and he told my mom he thought I was dead.

In those moments after impact, or perhaps during the next twenty-one days while I was in a coma, I had a near-death experience and saw Jesus. And to this day, I can remember that out-of-body experience as if it just happened.

Just as others have experienced, I was walking down a tunnel toward a bright light that looked like a cloud. When I came out of the tunnel, it was as if I was in the middle of a cloud with no walls, floor, or ceiling. The atmosphere was that of a very dense fog, but the mist that filled the air was almost golden in color, as if the fog was made of microscopic flecks of gold. I was in total peace as I walked toward what appeared to be a car in the middle of this brilliant fog. It was the exact same color and style of our car, only smaller. As I approached, I saw a tall figure standing beside the car with his right hand placed on top of the passenger side.

The magnificent figure was facing me, waiting for me to approach. I knew it was Jesus by the long, sheer white robe and long brown hair. As I stood in front of Him and His bare feet, I was mesmerized. I looked up at Him, but His face only appeared as a ball of light. His beautiful long, brown, wavy hair framed the light. As He stood there with His hand on the car, He spoke these words: "I am not ready for you to die yet. I have something special for you and your family on earth."

I do not know how long this out-of-body experience lasted or how I got back, but twenty-one days later when the brain swelling had subsided enough, I woke up. I later learned I had been sandwiched between the front and back seat during the accident. They had to use the Jaws of Life to get me out of the mangled car. I know now why my mother hadn't been projected through the open door at impact, and my body was not damaged in any way—Jesus had his hand on that car protecting us.

Some of the first words I spoke to the nurse in my room were, "Saw Jesus. Jesus pretty." During the weeks I was regaining my physical, verbal, and motor skills, my parents said that I would not stop telling the nurses and doctors about how I saw Jesus. They later told my parents that my recovery was a miracle. Two months after coming home from the hospital, I started fourth grade as a healthy child. Though I will never know, maybe that situation witnessed to those doctors and nurses.

Satan had tried to destroy my life, but God had other plans. My mom still has scars on her arm from the glass that was surgically removed, but I only have one tiny scar on my arm from the IV that fed me for three weeks.

A ROCKY ROAD AHEAD

After the accident, my parents' marriage coasted along for the next four and a half years, but they divorced when I was fourteen. I thank God He watched over me during my teenage years as I tried to cope with the pain of my parents' divorce.

At the end of my eleventh grade year, I pulled back from the rowdy group of friends whose partying ways were no longer ideal for the direction I wanted to take my life. I got involved in my church youth group, and after graduating, God led me to a Christian university where I learned what it really meant to have a relationship with Him and to know the power of the Holy Spirit.

Those four years of college prepared me spiritually to know how to rely on my relationship with God to get through hard times. I just wish someone would have taught me what it meant to have *an identity in Christ* and to be whole in Christ during those early adult years. Had I known those truths, the trauma I faced at twenty-four would have steered me down a totally different road than the one I chose.

CHAPTER 1: A SECOND CHANCE AT LIFE
REFLECTION QUESTIONS:

1. Relationship patterns can be generational. As you look back on your parents' and grandparents' relationships, do you see any positive or negative patterns that have been repeated in your own life? Explain.

2

My Fraudulent Prince Charming

For still the vision awaits its appointed time;
it hastens to the end—it will not lie. If it seems slow, wait for it; it
will surely come; it will not delay.
(HABAKKUK 2:3 ESV)

Isaiah 55:8 says that God's ways are not our ways and His thoughts are not like ours. There are times we think God's plan is unfolding for us, but it really is not. Something great comes along or a great opportunity presents itself, and we think because it is so great that it must be of God. But just because an opportunity smells right, looks right, and fits all your definitions of right, it doesn't mean that it is what God wants for you. That is why we have to ask for wisdom and discernment, because not all good situations are His plan. His ways are not always the ways we think we should walk in.

Have you ever been in a situation where you think it's a "God thing," and you think you have God's big picture all figured out, only to eventually realize you had it all wrong? Sometimes we think we know what God wants for us, but in time, we learn our thinking was not at all His plan.

After high school, I went to a Bible college called Lee University. When I became old enough to marry, I began to think that I would find my God-given purpose wearing the title of "minister's wife" or just "wife" period. My heart's greatest desire, beginning at age nineteen, was to be in ministry of some sort with the man I would marry. I longed for the fairy tale and used to believe that I would finally be fulfilled in life once I got rid of the title "single" and gained the recognition of a married woman. That dangerous mindset set me up to be a target. I remembered Jesus' words in that bright light, that He had something special for my family and me on earth. In my young, naive mind, I thought the "special thing" that God had for me and my family would be discovered once I married a man who had a heart and calling for ministry.

I completed my first year in college feeling so sure that God had brought me to a school where men were getting Bible and pastoral degrees because I really wanted to be a pastor or youth pastor's wife and help him in ministry. I thought I had God all figured out. After graduating with a teaching degree and a minor in Bible, I was ready to conquer the world for Christ. But there was just one problem—I was still single. I was discouraged that I had not met my forever-after during my college years and gotten engaged or married like so many of my friends did. I questioned why He didn't allow me to meet my prince minister like my heart desired.

The day I left my college town for the final time and headed to Nashville, Tennessee, to temporarily live with my mom (who had moved there during my sophomore year in college), I talked to God almost the whole two-hour trip. I began to wonder if I had missed something and messed up the calling that I thought God had for me.

For some reason, the sermons telling me Satan wants to create a constant battle in our minds never sank in. And Satan began to work in my mind on that drive. I began to think that perhaps I was too picky and had let "The One" get away. That day, Satan planted a fear in me that maybe I would never find a Christian man like I should have in college when I was surrounded by them.

Even though I had begun to experience an intimate walk with Christ, I did not know what it meant to find my identity in Him. Instead of seeking to find my identity as a single woman in Christ, I began to seek it in a job and in finding a man. Satan was ready to try once again to kill, destroy, and knock me down. This time it wasn't with a car accident—it was through my fear of being single. Even though I must have heard it in countless sermons at Bible college, I failed to realize that Satan will often disguise himself in beauty. Something that can seem so right can often be a trap of quicksand placed in our path. And I was about to walk right into a trap.

THE MULTILEVEL MAGNET

While waiting to get my teaching license, I answered a job ad to sell health products, and I attended a sales meeting led by a handsome thirty-year-old man named Eric. After a two-hour meeting, I got sucked into a new multilevel-marketing company with the driving goal being to build residual income so that I could be free to be in a ministry and not have to worry about a paycheck. I remember coming home from the first meeting and sitting on my bed, praying about what to do. To be honest, I rarely knew when God spoke to me, but in this prayer, I almost heard the audible voice of God as I sat on my bed. It was so strong that it shocked me. He spoke to me and said, "This is not what I have planned for you." I could not deny it was God, no doubt about it, but do you think I listened? No. Instead, I began to reason with God and explain to Him why it would be great to build a downline of people who would pave my way into financial freedom so I could go on mission trips or be a part of any ministry He led me to. I chuckle now when I think about my immaturity at actually trying to convince God that my plan was better than His plan.

Have you ever done that? Tried to reason with God as if we can change His plan, as if we know what is better for us than He does? I wish I would have listened to Him back then. He tried to warn me, but I quenched the Holy Spirit and followed my own will. I ignored the unsettling feeling put there by the Holy Spirit, and joined the company, full of ambition. Little did I know, Satan was in that situation disguised in beauty and promises.

One week into attending the meetings to learn the business, I met the handsome guy who had led the meeting the week before. He walked into that office in his expensive suit and watch like a living, breathing ray of sunlight. His magnetic personality and charming, handsome demeanor demanded attention. He began leading the sales meetings with his suave talent, and he seemed to have a confident gift of persuading people. He had the respect of all those who worked in that office. Charming and Suave should have been his middle and last name. And Fraud should have been his first.

As I got to know Eric better and heard him profess his Christian faith, I fell for him. We began dating, and I introduced him to my family. They loved his charismatic, witty personality and business mind. He also appeared to be a solid Christian man. He quoted Scripture and talked the Christian talk. They were happy that I had found a good man; at least he acted that way.

I was young and blinded by love and thought I had met Prince Charming. In a short period of time, we fell in love. I began to share his dream to start a Christian publication that showcased all the city churches: a "church directory." I thought this man was "The One" and that our Christian business would thrive. I would finally have a "ministry" with my husband like I thought God wanted me to have, for my family and me.

I was so in love that I missed all the red flags in his story. I never met his parents. He told me they had died in a car accident several years before. He also told me he had inherited more than a million dollars from his parents' insurance policy when they died and that he had invested most of it. I did not doubt him due to the brand-new car he drove and the expensive clothes he wore. In addition, it appeared logical that he had support, since he did not have a paying job. On one occasion, I saw an ATM receipt with a balance of $34,000. As most young, gullible girls would under the spell of love, I trusted everything he told me.

After three months of putting my efforts into the multilevel-marketing company and working an evening waitressing job, I began to join him in his efforts to start the Christian publication. After dating just six months, he asked me to marry him. My mother and father both approved of a long engagement. All of my family who met him thought highly of him and believed he was a solid, smart, levelheaded Christian man with tremendous business sense.

My mom, as well as my Christian upbringing, had instilled values in me when it came to having premarital sex. I had it set in my mind that I would save myself for marriage, and I was very proud of myself that I had waited. But it was getting too difficult to wait until the wedding night set for eight months away, so without telling anyone but my mom, we eloped, but still continued to plan the wedding of my dreams.

For those of us who are older, we can look back at the days of our young adulthood and wish we could undo some of the stupid decisions we made out of immature thinking. This is one of those situations for me.

Two months after we eloped, plans for the wedding were still underway. Establishing and launching our church directory publication was our career focus, and we had signed a contract on a large home under construction in a prestigious development. I was walking on cloud nine and feeling like Cinderella, when it all came to a screeching halt one Thursday evening in April.

MARRIED TO A STRANGER

I received a phone call from my brother, who was then a South Carolina state constable. He told me he became suspicious of Eric when he caught him in some lies on the telephone the day before. He did a background check on him and found that he did not exist under the name and date of birth that he claimed to have. This man was so skilled at being a con artist that he had a fake driver's license with his picture on it and the name he claimed.

My brother asked to speak to Eric, who was with me at that time. After the phone conversation, Eric grabbed his keys in anger and told me he was going for a drive to cool off. He walked out of the apartment we had just rented after we eloped, and I did not see him again until three weeks later . . . when he was in handcuffs. My brother did not get any confessions out of him when they spoke, but the next day he got in his car and drove up to Nashville to help his sister find out who her "husband" really was.

Despite the repeated attempts to contact him for answers on the night he left, he would not answer his phone. The next morning, the call finally came from the man I was calling my husband. His words to me were, "I am so sorry. I really do love you, but I did not know how to keep you out of this. I wanted to find a better life with you and really do something for God, but it is true. I am not who you think I am. I am living under someone else's identity."

He kept apologizing over and over again and finally hung up. My phone dropped to the floor along with my stomach. Alone in my state of shock, I began to sob and shake. I could hardly breathe because the emotions were so intense. At first I was in denial. This kind of thing didn't happen to girls like me! This seemed like something you see in the movies. But this is what God was trying to warn me about. He had known what I was about to walk into, and he had tried to warn me. The nightmare I had walked into could have been spared had I listened to God and not followed my own reasoning and emotions.

I thank God for my brother and mom being at my side to help keep me sane through the first few days of this horrific shock. My brother went with me to file a police report and held me up during the first days of intense stress. After two days of crying and searching through every home office file looking for puzzle pieces, I was able to pull myself together enough to share the situation with our custom home builder. In his own suspicions of me, he led me to the TBI (Tennessee Bureau of Investigations), where he asked them to investigate us both. After finding that I had a flawless background, they asked me to work with them to catch Eric, whose real name they discovered was John. As all the details the TBI found came to light, my brokenness turned into fear. Not only did this man have my entire family snowed, John was already wanted in four states for bank fraud. The bank in Franklin, Tennessee, where we had a business account, had just become his fifth state. John had stolen more than $10,000 from the bank the week before this discovery. Looking back, I see how God's timing and his use of my brother spared me from going to jail. My name was on the account with "Eric." I could have been arrested for fraud, but God spared me. God is always working and orchestrating even when we can't realize it.

The shock and stress of all that was transpiring, and all the plans I was left to undo, sent me into a temporary mental breakdown. Because I was married to him and also on the bank account, I was now considered an accomplice to this fraud I had no knowledge of. The only reason I was not arrested at the demands of the president of the bank was because the men at TBI believed I was innocent and told the bank president that I was in agreement to help them catch John.

Finally, after three weeks of suffering from anxiety attacks and sleeplessness, I was able to convince John to meet me on his terms. The morning of the meeting, I met with a team of TBI agents at 6 a.m. They put a body wire on under my clothes because that was the only method they had at the time to be able to hear my phone conversation with him as I drove alone in a car to meet him. As we drove out of Nashville headed toward Knoxville, which is the direction John told me to drive, I was surrounded by four cars of TBI agents. I remember feeling as if I were in the scene of a movie and wondering how I, of all people, ended up there. Although Satan tried to cripple me with fear and anxiety on that drive, a determination came over me that superseded the anxiety. I was not about to go to jail for a crime I did not commit!

When I finally arrived at the destination where John told me to meet him, he was already on the ground in handcuffs. The TBI had advised me to act really upset to throw John off, and so I did. If he knew I had set him up, they were afraid he might turn vengeful.

He confessed to the TBI agents on the drive back to Nashville that I had nothing to do with any of his criminal acts. John spent several years in prison, serving time in each of the five states where he had fraud charges. He found out after he was sent to jail that I had led the TBI to his arrest, and for many years I feared he might one day show back up in my life. I am thankful once again that God spared me and protected me. Other than letters sent to my mom's residence during the first three years he was in jail, I have never heard from him. As for me, the drama ended the day he was arrested, but it took months for me to piece together the life this man had destroyed.

If you are in a relationship or in the early stages of getting to know someone, and you start to have a gut feeling that something is not right, pay attention to it. Warning signs and unsettling feelings should not be ignored. Oftentimes they are warnings from God. He may be trying to spare you from something that only He can see in the future.

CHAPTER 2: MY FRAUDULENT PRINCE CHARMING REFLECTION QUESTIONS:

1. If you desire to marry, will you allow society or others to put pressure on you to get married in a certain timeframe or do you put pressure on yourself? If so, why?

2. Thinking back on your younger dating life, were there decisions you made that you thought were God-inspired at the time, but later were shown to be poor decisions? List them

here, as well as the outcome. What did you learn from those experiences?

3. Have you ever dated someone who did not turn out to be all that they appeared to be in the beginning? If so, how did you respond? Did you stay with them or walk away?

4. Have you ever seen red flags in someone or had an uneasy feeling about dating someone, but you continued to be with the person, only for it later to end badly? If so, what made you stay with the person and ignore the red flags? What will you do next time if you see red flags when dating someone?

3

Putting an Unraveled Life Back Together

*"Behold, I am the LORD, the God of all flesh;
is anything too hard for me?"*
(JEREMIAH 32:27 ESV)

After John's arrest, I was left with having to rebuild my entire life at the young age of twenty-four. In one month's time, I lost my marital status, a place to live, my car, access to any money we had in his account, the career I had started, and my good credit, which he had destroyed without my knowledge. I was left to undo all that we had started to build. It was embarrassing, to say the least. The marriage was annulled due to fraud. The leased Lexus went back, the apartment lease was terminated, the house contract was null and void with no return of the earnest money, and my virginity and self-worth were gone as well.

In the midst of my stress, I was bitter. I questioned why. *How could this happen to me? Why did I meet this one man out of all the people in Nashville?* I was angry at God. He could have stopped this man from crossing my path. And for a very long time, I was angry at myself for being so naive and for settling. I had ignored the warnings God had given me in the beginning. I chose the relationship anyway because it was what I wanted, not what God wanted. It all seemed so right except for the gut feeling that revisited me time and again. My wants and my own will overshadowed what the Holy Spirit was trying to tell me. John was not what God wanted for me, and He was trying to tell me, but I settled for him mainly out of fear that I would never find someone like him. Had I not settled, a huge mess could have been avoided, and the next twelve years of my life would have looked very different.

BACK TO SQUARE ONE

After John was arrested, it took me several weeks to gain enough mental stability to work. I moved back in with my mom, so I was thankful I was not homeless. My credit was such a mess that I had to file for bankruptcy. A church donated an old car with no AC to me, but I was thankful I could get back and forth to work once I got a new job. Slowly, over the next six months, I began to piece my life together.

Upon joining a church and making new friends, life seemed to be somewhat normal again; however, I was doing what so many others do. I stuffed my wounds, pretended they were not there, and continued to tell myself and everyone around me that I was strong and fine. But I wasn't fine. On the inside I was angry. I was angry at the man who had torn up the life I was trying to establish, and angry at myself for being so naive and continuing in a situation that *appeared to be right*. And I was angry that my mistake had led me to a place of brokenness.

I was no longer the same girl I was the day I left Lee University. I had been violated and shaken to the core by a crisis that I had brought upon myself. Instead of healing this anger, I buried it. I was empty inside, and part of me was lost. Of course I didn't want anyone to see what a wounded, insecure mess I was on the inside. Instead of running to my Savior to try to find myself in Him, I ran the other way. Relationships became my Band-Aid. This is a common thing many hurt single people do. They try to find someone or something to fill a void or to take their mind off their own pain instead of taking the time to heal. I realize now that not finding wholeness in Christ and establishing an identity in Him was perhaps an even bigger mistake than the one I was trying to get over.

My life became like a series of dominos, falling one after another. Our life can be like dominos if we are not careful and do not use wisdom. We start to become established and upright when we become young adults. And the enemy seeks us out and looks for the right moment to knock us down through damaging situations. If we do not recognize this and take action to do something to establish ourselves "upright" again physically, mentally, and emotionally, then we may end up falling or being knocked down time and time again. Then we end up in a place where we look back and see a defeated mess of our lives and wonder how we got there.

AND BABY MAKES THREE

After being swindled by a con man, I went through several short-term dating relationships and ended up pregnant out of wedlock. I married the father of my son, thinking it was the best thing to do. Once again, I had an unsettling feeling in my spirit. I had no audible warning from God, but I knew on my wedding day that our marriage would be rocky and might not last because of our personality differences. I continued of my free will and did what I felt was best for our child.

Through four of the five years of marriage, I watched my husband have an affair with drugs, pain pills, and alcohol. I had another unplanned child, and we had some sweet family times, but the bouts of dysfunction the young children had to witness were frightening me. After many attempts to work on the marriage, I finally left and chose the road of being a single mom. I could not bear any more of the dysfunction that stemmed from my husband's drug abuse, verbal abuse, and volatile personality the drugs created. I knew that if I didn't leave, my children would grow up repeating the cycle of dysfunction. While I am thankful he is drug free today, the personality differences and damage done were too great for us to reconcile.

It was hard being a single mom. I was lonely and missed the companionship of a man, so ten months after I filed for divorce, I went looking for love on two dating websites. I didn't think much anymore about the experience I'd had where Jesus told me He had something special for my family and me. I assumed I had missed it. I thought I had messed up my life so badly from following my own heart's desires to find love that I had disqualified myself at that point from being an effective person God could use to advance His kingdom.

Satan had me right where he wanted me. I was still in church and still praising the Lord, but I walked under a cloud of self-condemnation. All I cared about, as a broken and empty woman who was not whole, was finding a decent Christian man with a good job. I bought into the belief that not many men out there would want a woman with two kids. I actually told myself *I would have to settle* because I thought my chances were slim. I wish I would have made a U-turn in my mindset at the age of thirty-two, but I continued the cycle of following my own will, and I suffered even more consequences and heartaches. The dominos continued to fall for three more years. I only ended up feeling used and full of regret.

In the midst of my poor choices, I am so thankful God closed many wrong doors for me, so I did not miss what He had for my future. I thank Jesus for protecting me in my state of internal mess, while trying to find myself in the wilderness.

WHAT'S YOUR STORY?

So what avenue are you coming from? What has caused you to become frustrated with the single life? Are you unhappy with your dating track record? Are you trying to recover from a failed relationship? Are you sick of being lonely? Are you burned out and overwhelmed as a single mom? Are you still angry and bitter toward someone who hurt you? Do you want to become smarter and stronger in the dating arena and stop settling for unhealthy men? Are you tired of waiting?

Whatever your reason, there must be something in you that

you are realizing needs changing or healing. If there is anything in your life that needs changing, it has to first start on the inside. No other human being can change your situation. Only you can stand up in the midst of your circumstances and current mindset and force them to change, with the help of your heavenly Father.

Maybe your external circumstances won't change, but you can certainly change the way you choose to view them and how you allow them to affect you. You can also learn to block the enemy when he tries to beat you down in the midst of your everyday life.

It was the broken and defeated men and women in the Bible that He raised up and used to be examples for the world. No matter what you have experienced, remember that we have a God who can bring greatness from our mistakes. He will do what His Word says. He will make your life and your past beautiful in time (Ecclesiastes 3:11). The result is a stronger and more influential you. A benefit of God's greatness is giving you your heart's desires in His time. He will call forth the abundant life He longs to give you as you grow in Him. And part of that abundant life can be a beautiful way He uses you to impact the lives of others.

If our God can create man from dust, He can certainly create a beautiful life from the ashes of our failures and the wounds others have left behind.

CHAPTER 3: PUTTING AN UNRAVELED LIFE BACK TOGETHER REFLECTION QUESTIONS:

1. When life hasn't gone the way you hoped, how have you handled stress and disappointment?

2. What advice would you have for someone who faces heart-aches and trials?

3. We've all felt defeated at least a few times. When you're going through difficult times, to whom or what do you turn to for encouragement? If you have a favorite Bible verse that encourages you, list it below.

4

Try, Try Again

*"Be strong and courageous; do not be frightened or dismayed, for
the LORD your God is with you wherever you go."*
(JOSHUA 1:9 NRSV)

After almost three years of online dating, I finally figured out
that most of the men on dating websites were just as wounded as
I was on the inside. Like me, they were seeking a companion to
fill a void or make them forget about something they'd lost. I became weary of meeting different men, getting into short-term relationships, and having my hopeful heart squashed by men who
needed to work on their own issues themselves. On the outside
I appeared to have it all together, and so did the men I chose to
go out with. I realized that a lot of men can hide the skeletons in
their closet very well and act the way a woman wants them to
masking their true nature.

Done with online dating, I ran from the websites and ran into
more church functions. I went to all the singles functions my
church offered when my children weren't with me, and I even
went to friends' churches as well. My expectations of meeting
a man were placed in church. I figured if I was going to meet a
Christian man, it was going to be in church.

The final dating experience in the "wrong lane" was the clincher—the wake-up call to self-realization, and the situation that brought my ways and attempts to find the desires of my heart to a screeching halt.

BAD TO THE BONE

Jim had been attending my church for about six months. I met him one morning in the church café while waiting in line to get breakfast. He was an attractive, clean-cut man wearing jeans and a motorcycle vest. This guy did not fit the typical biker dude profile, but nevertheless I was intrigued by his friendliness and personality. I started talking to him about his ministry, and when I discovered there was no ring on his finger, my attention level became more intense. Since the café was full, we decided to share a table to eat. During the friendly conversation, I was drawn in by his witty and outgoing personality and his zeal for God. Telling me he was a graduate of Oral Roberts divinity school and the pastor of a motorcycle ministry, he definitely grabbed my attention. He even pulled out his phone to show me a picture of him in a cap and gown standing next to Oral Roberts. It was certainly believable.

We discussed motorcycles and how much I once enjoyed riding one with my ex-husband. His response was what I was hoping for: "When I have some free time, I will take you." We friended each other on Facebook. A week later he messaged me and told me his available weekend times. On a weekend in May when I didn't have my kids, an afternoon motorcycle ride was the start of a six-week dating experience.

His ability to preach, sing, play piano, and write encouraging messages on his ministry website made it easy for me to think I may have found a keeper. After all, he appeared to be the total package. *And I met him in church!*

I had more time to date while I was off in the summer and when my children were gone to their father's house. The first few weeks of dating we were able to spend a great deal of time together. I was amazed at the talents this man had and his heart for ministry. Of course I began to think that maybe this was the man I was supposed to have a ministry with. A motorcycle ministry had never crossed my mind, but since my heart's greatest desire had been to have a ministry with the man I marry, I had an open mind. Little did I know that this situation was one more trap intended by the enemy to derail my life.

GUT CHECK

About six weeks into this dating experience, I was having coffee on my couch one morning, reading a devotion, when I began to have the most disturbing feeling in my gut—it was the same feeling I had had on my bed years before when I'd heard God speak to me. I was struck with fear that something was terribly wrong, and the feeling didn't leave me for days.

At first I passed it off as me being afraid of getting hurt again, but when Jim canceled two dates with me for a "ministry" purpose that week, that unsettling feeling turned into a warning in my spirit that something wasn't right. This time I decided to pay attention to the Holy Spirit. Thank God for the Internet and the ability to do background checks!

As I began to do some research on this man and his ministry, I found all sorts of complaints posted. A few clicks later, and his name came up on a sex offender registry in another state. I also discovered he had spent some jail time in another state for theft. *Not again!* To make matters more difficult, I discovered that he was dating another girl at church while dating me. All of this was heartbreaking to learn, and it greatly angered me that this man preached the Word to homeless people and motorcycle gangs, yet he was deceiving people. Luckily, I got away with no devastating consequences. He never came back to the church we attended. After this experience, I went on one more blind date, but it was uneventful and that was the end to my single lane of running from myself and searching for love my way. Finally giving up on dating, I began to do a lot of soul searching and self-reflection.

I wondered if there was something wrong with me that I attracted these deceptive men. Did I wear a sign on my head that only men could see that read "Desperate and Dateless"?

It was through the shame and disappointment of failed relationships that I finally came to the end of myself and laid my unraveled life of codependency, shame, regret, and disappointment at the feet of Jesus. I regretted that I had given myself sexually to different men, but I asked God to forgive me and restore me, and He did. However, forgiving myself was harder. I battled against soul ties that had been created through intimacy with those men, and those ties were broken in Jesus' name. In my tears and prayers through those few weeks I was at "rock bottom," God reminded me that He is constant. His Word never changes, nor do His promises. He sees our life from the beginning to the end. He knows the mistakes that we will make in our life from the time we are born. Our sins and our failures don't shock Him. He never stops seeing us through eyes of mercy.

Because God has given us free will, it is up to us to choose the roads we will travel. He will never force us to pursue Him or to find healing and wholeness in Him. It is up to us to pursue the truth. I believe God did want me to go in another direction after I graduated from Lee University, and my choices took me down a road He never intended me to travel. But the awesome thing about our God is that His name is Redeemer. He has already planned an awesome life beyond our mistakes if we follow Him.

He is not a God who keeps a record of our wrongs and holds our past against us. He does not condemn us. It is the enemy who wants us to condemn ourselves. God doesn't look at what we have done. He sees the woman He longs for us to be. He never stops offering amazing strength, joy, contentment, and wholeness that can be found only in Him. We need only to seek Him.

"If you look for me wholeheartedly, you will find me."
(JEREMIAH 29:13 NLT)

In my conversation with God, after the "pastor disaster" experience, I began to ask Him for help. My prayer went something like this: "Lord, I feel like I have made a mess of my life. I have

Section Two:
Gaining the Right
Perspective

*Trust in the LORD with all your heart and do not lean on your
own understanding. In all your ways acknowledge Him, and He
will make your paths straight.*
(PROVERBS 3:5–6 NASB)

5

The Awesome Single Woman: Wonderfully and Powerfully Made

*Praise the LORD! Happy are those who fear the LORD . . . They
are not afraid of evil tidings;
their hearts are firm, secure in the LORD.
Their hearts are steady, they will not be afraid.*
(PSALM 112:1, 7–8 NRSV)

I am guessing there is something you do not like about your
state of life in the "single lane," a road that is often filled with all
sorts of emotions. If we all got real with one another in a moment of truth, I wonder how many of us would say that we don't
like being single. We have to learn to cope, and we have fun experiences with friends, taking trips and going on single-life ad-
ventures, but at the end of the day, most of us want to be in a
relationship or married.

Who doesn't want to find a euphoric romance and grow old
with someone in a nice home with a nice yard on the corner
of Promise Street and Happy Lane? As little girls, many of us
grew up playing the princess who finds her prince and Barbie
who meets Ken. They have a dreamy romance and get married
and move into the Barbie Dream House. Finding love and romance seemed to be programmed into us at an early age. The

Cinderella and *Beauty and the Beast* stories we watched when we were young built on our ideals of love and romance.

Finally, at a certain age in life, we started to send out search signals and walk around with a love radar in our purse. We started to wonder where our Ken was. *When will he come and whisk me away and put an end to my lonely days?* And this love radar, buried in our purses, seems to never run out of batteries, even if we try telling ourselves it has.

Even if you are a single person who is focused on building a career and becoming established in life before you settle down or get into something long term, there is still that desire deep within to be loved and to share yourself with someone. We can't help but feel that way simply because God designed us for relationships.

There is absolutely nothing wrong with you if you long for love. Pay attention to where that longing leads you though. Our longing for love becomes *dangerous* when it drives us to become desperate or to settle. How many single people do you know who have gone through bad relationships and will tell you now that they knew the *whole time* they were with the person that it wasn't the best thing? Or maybe they admit that they don't know where their brain and self-respect were to stay with the person as long as they did. I know that scenario all too well. Maybe you do too!

After I divorced, in my desperation to fill a void from a man's desire for me, I ended up settling a few times. I got involved in relationships that I knew were not what God wanted for me. When they ended, they only left me with more scars and more regret to get over.

Maybe you can relate to me. Maybe you have also made choices that you wish you would not have, and now you are filled with regret. Even so, your past is in the past. Do yourself a favor and leave it there. There is nothing you can do to change what has already happened or undo choices already made. Turn any regret you may have into thankfulness. You can't take back mistakes, but you can thank God for what you learned or are learning from them. Thank Him for the strength and wisdom that He is building in you. Praise God that you may not be who you want to be now, but you are certainly not who you used to be. And you are not going to be the same from here forward. With every life experience, we gain wisdom, and more character is built in us.

Also thank God that He went before you and closed a door that you may not have closed yourself. Sure, failed relationships hurt, but keep believing your heavenly Father is working it all out for your good. There were many nights I cried over closed doors that I didn't want shut, but I now thank the good Lord for saving me from disasters I couldn't see. He knew what He had in store for me. Had I forced doors open that He had shut, I would have missed out on the jewel He had waiting for me.

You may not be able to change the fact that you are still solo, but you can find a new perspective. As with most things in life, if you want a change, it has to first start within.

A CHANGE FROM WITHIN

While you are waiting on the Lord for His best for you, take the time to focus on becoming the best woman you can be for Jesus and also for your future mate. When you want God to change your life, He can and He will, but not without intentional effort on your part as well. Does a soldier go out to fight in a war without preparing? Could a soldier win a battle without training and strengthening him or herself? Absolutely not. It is the same with our lives. We cannot become who we want to be and be a victorious single or married person if we do not train our minds and hearts for the struggles we face.

Ladies, you have to understand that a man cannot rescue us, complete us, be our happiness, or end our loneliness. Marriage does not guarantee an end to loneliness. I hear often from people in marriages that they still experience loneliness. Jesus is the only one who can satisfy the deepest parts of us.

The only way we can conquer our life struggles and burdens is to become secure in our own self-worth and secure in Him. When you make Jesus your all, find your contentment in Him, and look to the Holy Spirit to give you strength when you are lonely, you will become the strong and mighty daughter of God

He longs for you to be. No, life will not be perfect and struggle-free, but when Jesus becomes your heavenly Husband, the ultimate Lover of your soul, and the One you find contentment in, you will find the ability through Him to rise up and face each emotion and challenge as a single woman and later a married woman, if marriage is what you desire.

> *But they that wait upon the Lord shall renew their strength. They shall mount up with wings like eagles; they shall run and not be weary; they shall walk and not faint."*
> (ISAIAH 40:31 TLB)

A SOCIETY OF SINGLES

Times have drastically changed in the last sixty years. We have evolved into a fast-paced society where technology opens the world to us with the touch of a button, and we live in a day and age now where women are learning to take charge and seize their womanhood. In the last several decades or so, our society has gone from "You are considered an old spinster if you're not married by thirty" to "Good for you that you are building your career and getting the most out of life before you settle down!"

A woman's value and status used to be tied to her role as wife. Sixty years ago a woman could not open a bank account without her husband's signature. It used to be a man's world. Thank God times have changed! There are plenty of women who are putting themselves first and the wedding ring second, and there is nothing wrong with that. More and more women are choosing to be single now until later in life. We are in a seismic shift of the definition of single independent adulthood. But in spite of all these shifts, the longing to "find a significant other" still comes into play *eventually*. Aside from establishing a career and the gift of childbirth, marriage is the biggest rite of passage for a woman.

With this modern shift has also come the change in family and marital ideals and structures. We live in a society now where single adults are almost equal in number to married couples.

Here are some shocking statistics according to the US Census Bureau's Current Population Survey in 2010 and 2012:

- As of 2012, there were 112 million unmarried people over age 18 in the United States, representing nearly 47% of the adult population.
- In 2010, unmarried households were 45% of all US households.
- And in 2010, 44.9% of the unmarried population aged 18 and older were female![1]

I believe single women fall into one of the three categories below. See if one of these sounds like your inner dialogue.

1. "I hate being single. I am always seeking to find love and happiness."
2. "I am okay most of the time being single, but I am still searching for someone to share my life with."
3. "I am focused on my relationship with God, myself, and my career. I do not allow my past to define me, and I do not let the unknown future worry me. I am totally fine being single. When I am meant to meet someone, I will. Until that time comes, I will be about His business."

The last of those three categories is obviously the healthiest one to be in. But if you are a single mom falling into one of those categories above, you have a plethora of emotions to add into the equation! When you are a mom, it is no longer about your desires alone. Everything you do affects your children, and you are responsible for raising them to become productive and well-balanced adults. You must make good choices because if you don't, the mistakes you make will affect your children.

As a single woman, our goal should be to belong in category three. And yes, it is very difficult to make that change, especially when we deal with emotions brought on by the reminders of love all around us. But when we can get to that mindset and truly be content while we wait on the Author of our life to finish His story, we will find the strength and wisdom we need to overcome the obstacles that we face.

STRONGER THAN YOU REALIZE

I do not know how old you are or what your past looks like. But regardless of where you are in life right now, I commend you. I commend you for wanting to take charge of your life, for wanting to rise above and beyond your past, and for wanting to make the rest of your days in this season of life the best days. Hear me when I say this: Single Woman, Daughter of the most high God, you are strong! He put strength in you.

You can face the times of loneliness, when you spend weekends alone, because He will sustain you. You can get through the times of hurting and longing for a companion, because He is your Comforter, and a Father who has a master plan and destiny waiting for you. You can pick yourself up after you make a mistake or feel the disappointment with a date, because He is merciful and He knows a better plan for you than you have for yourself (Jeremiah 29:11). And you can fill your life with things besides a man to bring you fulfillment, because you have a purpose.

It took a lot of mental work, but I praise Jesus for what He taught me on the single road. He walked me through an amazing healing and growth process where I had to learn to find my identity and self-worth in Him. There are still days I battle with the enemy who wants to rob me of my strength and contentment, but Christ is my anchor. And He has and still is teaching me to be an overcomer. He defines my life. My purpose became all about Him and not in finding an end to my singlehood. When I finally learned to make Him my all and walk in a faith-filled mindset, I believe He finally saw I was ready, so He could begin to unfold the plan He wanted for me. And I learned that I am stronger than I ever knew I could be.

SALUTE THE SINGLE WOMAN

So we are single. So what! We should all salute the single woman.

She is *brave* for walking alone in this world.

She is *bold* for being the sole leader of her destiny.

She is *wise* for making her own choices.

She is *strong* for waking up every day and facing the responsibilities of life on her own.

She *has guts* to pull her comforter over her head night after night with no one beside her.

She is *admirable* for finding an identity in herself and not in the efforts of another.

She is *determined* because she puts on the cloak of perseverance every day.

You are and will be a strong single woman. Wear your single season with confidence and pride. Do not let your circumstances define your life! You can take charge, and you define it.

As you face each day solo, keep pressing on to find the strength and confidence to make the rest of this season of your life the best season of your life, so that the next season will be even better!

MIRROR MESSAGES

I am big on motivational sayings and posting encouraging words around my house and workplace. The more positive sayings I know, as well as uplifting Scripture, the more "comebacks" I have when I get down or when the enemy wants to start working in my mind. We all need a little pep talk from time to time, even if we're talking to ourselves! Cut out the sayings below and post them on your mirror, or write them on sticky notes and put them where you will see them during the day. When those thoughts creep in that tend to force you into a single pity party, build yourself up with these sayings as well as others you find that encourage you:

- I don't need another human being to complete my existence. The most profound relationship I will ever have is the one between my God and me.
- My life and state of identity do not define me. I define my life by the choices I make and who I choose to be.
- If I am not happy being single, then I won't be happy when I'm in a relationship. I know that true happiness comes from within and from my God, not from anyone else.

*"The strength of a woman is not measured
by the impact that her hardships and circumstances
in life have had on her. Her strength is found in a mindset
and refusal to allow those hardships and circumstances to dictate
who she is and who she becomes."*
—C. JOYBELL C.

CHAPTER 5: THE AWESOME SINGLE WOMAN: WONDERFULLY AND POWERFULLY MADE REFLECTION QUESTIONS:

1. The movies we watched as kids often gave us unrealistic expectations of what a relationship should look like. Think of one of your favorite childhood movies and write down a few main points about the lead characters' relationship.

   a. Now, thinking about that same movie, list three reasons as to why that fictitious relationship wouldn't really work in real life, or how it gives the wrong message to children about love.

2. We often feel like we are incomplete and worthless without a significant other or a spouse. But that is simply not true! We can be complete and know our worth is in Jesus Christ. Below, list ten things you like about yourself and four strengths that you have. Begin each line with "I like my..." or "One of my strengths is...."

3. When you are done with this list, find at least one Scripture in the Bible that tells you how worthy you are in the eyes of God.

4. What's your Mirror Message? Select an encouraging message from the bulleted list of motivational sayings or make your own. You can Google motivational sayings and find some great ones. Write them below and make sure you place a copy of your messages where you will see them every day.

6

Discovering Your God-Given Strength

"Do not grieve, for the joy of the LORD is your strength."
(NEHEMIAH 8:10 NIV)

When you go through the loss of a relationship, a marriage, a family, or longtime companionship, you feel like there is a big hole in the core of who you are. Your life has shifted while dealing with the loss, and you have to rediscover who you are without the other person. Having to learn to live life on your own again, especially if the relationship was lengthy, is one of the hardest challenges to face.

Even though I left my marriage of five years because I wanted peace, there were many nights I cried after my kids went to bed. I hated being a single mom at first because it felt unnatural, and there was no longer a man in the home to say goodnight to my kids. It constantly felt like something was missing; I know my kids felt this too. I had to adjust to being the only name my children called on to help them. I also had to adjust to doing everything for them on my own, and it was exhausting. I had to adjust to doing life totally on my own and never having a moment to myself until the kids were in bed. I felt burned out almost daily.

In the midst of having to adjust, I was grieving inside over the loss of a family for my children, dealing with guilt and anger, loneliness, resentment, and many more emotions. Despite the emotional turmoil I was in, I had to force myself to be strong for my kids and the fifty fifth graders I taught as a full-time schoolteacher.

How did I do it? I knew I had no choice. I had to learn that I could not operate in my own strength. I had to find spiritual and mental strength. My children were dealing with their own adjustments over the loss of a family, and I knew having a broken-down mom would make it harder on them. So I forced myself to wear a mask of strength. I tried to fake it until I made it. It was hard, and I failed often. Unfortunately, there were some days when I couldn't hold back the tears that came from feeling overwhelmed, and my kids did see me cry. But I explained that sometimes mothers just need to cry to release bottled-up emotions.

There were days when I just didn't know how to be strong. I was a mess inside. I kept telling myself that I was strong and Jesus was my strength and that I had no choice. I had to get up, put Amy to the side, and focus on the tasks in front of me. At night behind closed doors, I collapsed into the arms of Jesus.

I had lost my own identity while being married. My identity had been that of a wife and mother for five years, and now I was forced to find a new identity as a single woman and single mom. It wasn't easy, especially when I had to recover from even more disappointment when I started dating. Had I stopped dating sooner than I did, I could have saved myself a lot of emotional turmoil.

When I finally hit rock bottom almost three years after the divorce, I felt so broken. I had thought that I was strong at one time in my life, but through all my heartache and turmoil, I forgot what it even felt like to be strong. So I decided to create a vision statement of strength for my life. I would list out the many traits of the kind of woman I *wanted to be* and *needed to be*, so I would have a goal to focus on. It then became my mission to become this woman of strength.

I researched and asked some people at my church and in my workplace what they thought it meant to be a strong woman. I recorded several of the answers I heard; then I combined my favorite statements and posted them on my mirror. I read them daily until these truths became ingrained in me as my goal. I encourage you to create your own statements that can help you be stronger in Christ.

- A woman of strength has faith that she will become stronger during this journey.
- A strong woman won't let anyone get the best of her. Yet she gives the best of herself to everyone.
- A strong woman will persevere, regardless of the odds and circumstances. No matter how many times she stumbles, her faith and strength remain intact.
- A strong woman knows how to keep her life in order. Despite the struggle, she still manages to focus on her goals.
- A strong woman can carry mental and emotional weight. She can persevere when things get tough. She can dig deep into her faith reservoirs and know all things will work together for her good. She prays for more strength, and she seeks help in times of need.
- A strong woman has a strong sense of who she is; therefore, she's not swayed by public opinion.
- She protects her joy and peace. She covers her family and friends. And she stands up for what is right, even if she has to stand all by herself.
- A strong woman will not allow herself to be dominated by anyone's will or opinions. She takes control of her own destiny.
- A strong and virtuous woman has moral excellence and possesses admirable qualities. Strong women will make the most of a difficult situation.
- A strong woman will influence people around her through her actions and attitude. She is kind and confident. She is levelheaded and wise. She knows the influence she has on others and is determined to positively impact others around

her through her life actions.

- A strong woman respects herself and is comfortable being who God created her to be. Strong women know their worth.
- A strong woman understands that her identity is in God and that her spirit can be effective and highly influential.

Do I live a life of total strength and have this mindset every day? No. I am human and I fail. But when I fail, get down on myself, let my emotions get the best of me, or start to have a pity party, I read the attributes of a strong woman and recommit to myself that this is my life's goal.

It is up to you to become the woman you want to be. No one else defines your life but you and Jesus. You are a daughter of the most high God, His creation, His masterpiece. Do you know how He sees you? Flawless. Amazing and gifted. He sees you as the beautiful woman you can be. You are an investment to Him. He formed in you gifts and talents that He wants to use to glorify Him.

BY HIS DESIGN

One of the hardest things to do is see ourselves through the eyes of Christ, and others, for that matter. If we want to be a strong woman, single or married, we have to continually view ourselves the way God sees us—as His masterpiece.

No matter what you have come from, or where you have been, God is longing for you to rise up, take hold of Him, and walk in the beauty and strength He designed you to have. Women have so many God-designed and God-given abilities and inner strengths. You may feel like you are wearing a sign that says, "Depressed and Messed-Up Failure." And I should know because I have been there! But I finally took it off and refused to let the enemy keep flashing it in front of me. I stood up in the midst of my current situation, as a divorced single mom, and took hold of the strength and boldness that God wanted to give me.

You can face anything with your God, who can part oceans and walk on water. You may have moments of frustration and want to pull your hair out or cry, but God knows your frustration and every hurt you feel. Each day is a new day! Do not let your past hold your future ransom. Find your inner strength and focus on your Redeemer, the One who makes you strong.

God has the ability to take your past experiences and use them to strengthen you and give you a wisdom that you can use to bless others. For almost twelve years I allowed my past failures to inflict labels on me. I was stuck in a pit made by my own mindset. I finally decided that I would wear the labels Christ had for me and run full speed ahead to design my future in Him, simply because I wanted to be a better woman for God, myself, my loved ones, and the future plans that I trusted He had for me. I continually have the mindset to become that strong woman He is calling me to be. You need to have that mindset too.

PROVERBS 31 WOMAN

Have you ever read Proverbs 31? There are books out there about becoming the Proverbs 31 woman. Some of us get irritated at that Scripture because it seems like the woman that God wants us to be is a superwoman wife. Even though it is directed toward a "wife of noble character" and pointing out her worth, I want to challenge you to see this Scripture in a different light. Yes, God calls women to procreate and be wives and moms, but even if God has not positioned you in that role yet, that Scripture is still for you. The Proverbs 31 woman is God's way of saying to us that we as women are designed with gifts and abilities for a reason and purpose *no matter what our marital status is.*

What makes this nameless, yet famous, woman so significant is not the fact that she knows how to cook, make clothes, keep a clean home, have babies, and take care of her family. It's not the fact that she has great wisdom and business sense and seems to be a champion at everything. Of course, that's great and valuable for any godly woman, but it's her fear of the Lord that makes her a woman of virtue. Her perfection doesn't come from her home-making skills; it comes from her inner strength and mindset. Her abilities and strengths are not found within her own self-abilities. Her strength is found in her Maker: the One who owns her soul.

The only reason the Proverbs 31 Woman can be perceived as "perfect" is because she is a product of the God who lives within her. The only thing that's perfect about her is Him. She gets up every morning and perseveres in spite of her situation. She is able to persevere by depending on the strength that God has made available to her through Him. What makes her noble is she leans on the Lord to be her helper. She finds her worth and value in Him. She finds her purpose in her Lord. And ladies, as single women and single moms, we can find our value, purpose, and strength in our Lord. We may feel we stand alone in the world's eyes because we do not have a husband, but we can stand tall and strong in the identity of Christ, who has created us and called us to be women of noble character.

The woman in Proverbs 31 is the blueprint of the God-given abilities we all have, married or unmarried. She doesn't place her hope in her husband, her family, or her looks, but in God. Because of her fear of the Lord, she is able to be all that she is. As a result of her relationship with her Savior, she's an example to every woman who wishes to please the Lord because she fears Him first and foremost, and every other area of her life flourishes because of it.

As you read this Scripture, I want you to write or speak your name into the places where it says "her," "she," or "wife." I've added my own notes in brackets throughout the verses.

Proverbs 31:10–31 NIV

A [woman] of noble character who can find?

[Your name] is worth far more than rubies.

[Your name]'s [future] husband [and everyone she influences] has full confidence in her and lacks nothing of value.

[Your name] brings him good, not harm, all the days of her life.

[We can bless others with our abilities.]

[Your name] selects wool and flax and works with eager hands.

[God gives us wisdom and talents to earn a living.]

[Your name] is like the merchant ships, bringing her food

from afar.

[We can be resourceful and find the good in difficult places.]

[Your name] gets up while it is still night; she provides food for her family and portions for her female servants.

[Even under difficult situations, God gives us the ability to care for others.]

[Your name] considers a field and buys it; out of her earnings she plants a vineyard.

[God can give us financial wisdom to provide for ourselves and our children.]

[Your name] sets about her work vigorously; her arms are strong for her tasks.

[We don't give up when things get uncomfortable. Our strength pushes us forward.]

[Your name] sees that her trading is profitable, and her lamp does not go out at night.

[Even when we are tired, we press on knowing people depend on us.]

In her hand [your name] holds the distaff and grasps the spindle with her fingers.

[We know how to be productive.]

[Your name] opens her arms to the poor and extends her hands to the needy.

[God gives us compassion to help those in need and reach out beyond ourselves.]

When it snows, [your name] has no fear for her household; for all of them are clothed in scarlet.

[We have the innate instinct to rise up and protect and take care of the ones we love, especially during hardship.]

[Your name] makes coverings for her bed; she is clothed in fine linen and purple.

[We know how to make ourselves shine and look divine.]

[Your name] is clothed with strength and dignity; she can laugh at the days to come.

[We can lean on the Lord for strength and walk in faith that He holds our future.]

[Your name] speaks with wisdom, and faithful instruction is on her tongue.

[God will give us the boldness and wisdom to lead our family, children, and friends.]

[Your name] watches over the affairs of her household and does not eat the bread of idleness.

[When there is a job to be done, we don't settle for laziness.]

[Your name]'s children arise and call her blessed; her husband also, and he praises her:

[God wants us to make an influential impact. He knows the influence we have over children and men.]

"Many women do noble things, but you surpass them all."

[A woman whose character shines with the love and strength of Jesus is an admirable woman.]

Charm is deceptive, and beauty is fleeting; but a woman who fears the LORD is to be praised.

[Our worth comes from the woman God made us to be on the inside. Our character and inner beauty should be what others see and praise.]

Honor [your name] for all that her hands have done, and let her works bring her praise.

When I read Proverbs 31, I can see that God created women to be awesome! This verse challenges me to be a better woman! He has gifted us with the innate abilities to be so very influential and strong. The problem is that so many of us had childhoods that never nurtured these God-given abilities. Some of us had painful upbringings. Then when we became adults and went through more painful situations, some of these innate abilities were further quashed. We lost sight of them.

It is not man who defines us. It is not an ex-husband, an ex-boyfriend, or a parent. No matter what negative words you have heard from those who did not have their hearts in the right place, the only words that should influence you are the words of your Creator.

When we rise up and become the women God wants us to be, He will honor us and bless us. As women we can have a powerful positive influence on the lives around us.

If you ever need a reminder about how wonderful your future can be, post Matthew 7:11 and Hebrews 11:1 on your wall or write them in your journal: "Faith is confidence in what we hope for and assurance about what we do not see" (Hebrews 11:1 NIV). When I look at Hebrews 11:1, what stands out to me is 1–1–1. I see it as Father, Son, and Holy Spirit make three! They hold your future. We can't see it, but they can. We hope for what we can't see, and while we hope, we walk in assurance that the Father is leading us. That is what it means to walk in faith.

So keep choosing to get up, dust off the blues and feelings of loneliness, and move forward. And be careful to not allow self-pity to enter your mind. When we focus on what we don't have more than what we do have, it can force us into a pit that may be hard to get out of. So as hard as it is, keep walking in faith!

You have a God who loves you and says, "I have come that they may have life, and have it to the full" (John 10:10 NIV). God wants to greatly bless you, but there is a time He chooses to do it. So if you are frustrated with being single, don't think God is withholding an abundant future from you to be cruel. There is a master plan that only He knows, and all we can do is walk in faith knowing that He holds the blueprints.

LED BY GOD, NOT EMOTIONS

Each day is a gift if you choose to make it. Yesterdays are gone, but you have a day and future in front of you to make a difference. Each day is an opportunity to start over.

Do not allow yourself to get stuck and operate your life through emotions such as loss and bitterness. It is understandable to grieve with any loss. Take time to grieve and then move forward. Operate your life through the strength that Christ has given you. Don't just exist as a single woman trying to live through a mundane life until you "find the one who completes you." There is no voice but your own that tells you what you can and can't be. Your life is what you choose to make it. Choose to exist as an amazing, strong, single woman operating through her

Savior while you are making the most of each day and walking in faith.

It is a mindset! You can be as strong as you tell yourself you are. Even if you don't feel strong, tell yourself over and over again that you are simply because you have Christ in you and He makes you strong. We've heard the saying "fake it till you make it." Well, I am telling you to *believe it till you become it!*

Post your vision statement of strength on your mirror and read it every morning. Your strong inner self is there—you just have to find her and welcome her into the world.

CHAPTER 6: DISCOVERING YOUR GOD-GIVEN STRENGTH
REFLECTION QUESTIONS:

1. Think about a time when you experienced a loss, whether through divorce, death, illness, or another unforeseen event. While processing this loss you probably experienced times where you didn't feel very strong, although you had to still function in daily life. List two things you did every day that helped add structure or gave you the ability to persevere through the days of an otherwise chaotic time.

2. In trying times, how do you process your emotions? Do you journal? Do you spend time in nature? Do you sing? Do you pray or read the Bible? List at least three examples below. Also list two things you *could* do that you haven't already done.

3. What is *your* definition of a strong woman? What kind of woman are you and what kind of woman do you want to be? Take a few moments and create a definition for yourself. This definition should reflect the strengths that you have and those you want to have. Even if you do not feel this way about yourself now, write down several attributes you want to work toward. If you need to, use the bullet points in the chapter to help you form your own statement of strength.

7

Beware of Expectations

*"If you, then, though you are evil, know how to give good gifts to
your children, how much more will your Father in heaven give
good gifts to those who ask him!"*
(MATTHEW 7:11 NIV)

My dear friend Kim was an inspiration to me as I was walking
through my years of heartache and consequences. She graduated
from Lee University unmarried (like me), and eventually moved
on her own to Nashville. She spent ten years of her life serving in
church, getting a master's degree in divinity, becoming ordained,
and working as a staff member at a large church.

During our friendship, many times she shared with me her
frustrations of having to wait. God spared her at one point from
going down the wrong road, and even after several years of being
single in ministry, she still had an amazing faith that God would
give her the desires of her heart. She did not want to run ahead
of His plan for her life. She trusted in His timing even though it
was hard.

Then, at thirty-six years old, she reconnected with a man she
had known at the church she had attended when she was younger. In fact, he had been in her youth group at a church her father
had pastored, and their parents had been good friends while they

can move forward in wholeness. You can heal through Christ! This is the season of your life, no matter how long it may be, to invest in you. Get off the dating websites and get into your own life. Get your mind right, your emotions right, your attitude right, your priorities right, and get your walk with Christ right if it hasn't been. That is how you become whole. When your life becomes totally reliant upon Christ to fulfill your every need and you have a close relationship with Him, you will walk in wholeness.

Maybe you can relate to my friend Miranda who has been waiting on God to bring someone into her life for eleven years. At twenty-five, she was left a single mom of a toddler, so she spent her time raising her son, educating herself, and growing in Christ. It has been eleven years since she has had a relationship. It is not because men don't desire her. It is because she is so focused in life that she doesn't want to make any mistakes, so she chooses to wait on God. She is an amazing Christian woman who is strong and whole in Christ. Now with a fourteen-year-old and working on a nursing degree, she tells me, "I'm tired of waiting. I am so ready to share my life with someone, but I have no choice but to wait." She questions why God hasn't brought someone into her life when she has been so faithful and dedicated to Him. My answer to her is, "Because He is still getting him ready."

IN THE MEANTIME . . .

You, Daughter of God, are also going to be a special gift that God gives to a man. In the process of weaving together your life and character, He is also weaving together the man's. When the two of you come together, you will be a part of a beautifully woven plan He has designed for both of you. When we take matters into our own hands to try and find a man through dating websites or other means, it will fail if both people are not whole and it is not God's design.

Instead of expecting and hoping to find love one day, start expecting your love to grow in Christ. Make your growth in character and in Christ your number-one expectation! Make this a season of life where you find the secret to true lasting contentment that no human being or earthly situation can offer. That true contentment is found in a close walk with Christ. His Spirit lives in us when we ask Him to come into our lives. That Spirit can and will engulf us when we long for it. It will comfort us, guide us, and fill us with a soul satisfaction that no one else can give.

So what do you do in the meantime? Spend your lonely evenings reading a book. Call it a "date with an author" if you must. There are so many amazing books out there by excellent authors such as Beth Moore, Joyce Meyer, Priscilla Shirer, Max Lucado, Charles Stanley, and more that can help you to build your faith and relationship with Christ.

Through reading, you learn and you grow and sharpen your skills. When I finally gave up looking and hoping for a man, I spent many Friday nights, when my children were gone, sitting alone on my couch. Worship music softly played in the background, lit candles filled the room with sweet scents, and I was curled up under a blanket with coffee and a book. I would ask the Holy Spirit to come and sit with me as I read and fill me with contentment. After many months of doing this, I began a single moms' group at my home. Not because I was an expert or thought I had spiritual qualifications. It was so we could challenge and encourage one another as we faced the journey together. My church did not have a single moms' support group or Bible study, so I just decided to be the change I wanted to see in that area, even if it was for only a season.

I am not saying that the multiple weekends I spent alone were easy. I had to fight feelings of loneliness many times throughout those weekends, and the enemy coming in my mind, trying to make me feel sorry for myself for not being out with friends or in a relationship. I would often verbally fight the enemy. "Satan, get behind me in the name of Jesus. This is my time, Devil. I am in God's training camp. You won't knock me down. I will continue to be a threat to you in the name of Jesus." And in the times I got down, I cranked the worship music up and began to praise Him.

Those weekends I spent with Jesus became so fulfilling that I began to look forward to them. I would read an entire book in a weekend and love it! In that year that I spent with just me, myself, and Jesus, I grew like never before. Jesus filled me with a soul satisfaction and contentment that no earthly man's love can give. I learned what it meant to become whole and content in Christ.

I never gave God a time limit. I just gave up on the idea of ever having someone in my life. It became a distant desire for me! I told God many times that if He wanted me to have someone, He would have to bring him in front of my face or to my door because I was no longer looking. I actually asked God to take away my desire for a companion.

I no longer saw a cute single man at my church and wondered if he could be the one. I no longer hoped to meet a man at a function I went to. I never went on a dating website again, and I never again asked for someone to set me up with a single friend if they had one. I stopped expecting. I got to a point where I was too afraid of making another mistake and messing up the amazing work God was doing in me. I didn't want to go through more dating experiences, and I certainly didn't want to risk my heart being broken again. What I began to expect was for God to orchestrate every step of my life. When and if He had a gift for me, He would orchestrate that too.

While on this journey of finding my life and identity in Christ, God prompted me to write this book. As I began to write, I got so busy with the single moms' group, functions at my church, and writing, that my desire for an earthly love totally left me. Perhaps that is what it means to be content. My life had total satisfaction. I didn't even care to have a man because I felt I had found such a fulfilling purpose as a single woman. I embraced my single journey with stride and grace. I remember telling God that I was okay and accepted it if I was to be single the rest of my life.

Now, I am not saying this was easy. To get to this level of contentment and to have this attitude coupled with no expectations for an earthly love took a lot of battling with Satan. He tried to work on my emotions and in my thoughts often, and I had to fight it with the Word of God and keep my perspective in check. I had to learn to control my thoughts in order to become the woman I longed to be. And I am still working on myself because it takes a lifetime to become a strong and effective woman of God.

I never imagined God would bring me a gift after a season of learning to be whole and content in Him. I had resigned myself to the possibility that I would raise my kids into their adulthood as a single mom, and I was okay with that. But God must have felt that I was ready and the man was ready, because he showed up in front of me when I no longer had expectations of finding love. And when he finally came, it made the years of doubt, rejection, heartache, and frustration fall away.

Until love finds you, enjoy growing in your gifts and growing closer with the Lord. And when rejection comes your way, you can learn to see it as a blessing of God's protection as you wait for the right one.

CHAPTER 7: BEWARE OF EXPECTATIONS REFLECTION QUESTIONS:

1. As young adults, we likely had a mental list of goals we wanted to achieve by a certain time in order to feel successful. Graduate college by twenty-two. Marriage by twenty-five. Two children and a house by thirty. List three of your life goals below.

a. Did you achieve them in the arbitrary timeframe you set for yourself?

b. If not, how has it made you feel?

2. Sometimes our man-made goals no longer serve our purposes and they hold us back. For every goal you haven't yet achieved, take time now to reevaluate it against God's timeline and set a new goal for yourself. For example, if you wanted to be married by the time you were twenty-seven and you just celebrated birthday twenty-nine as a single woman, perhaps a new goal for this year could be to go on a fun cruise with a group of friends, join an outdoor activities group, write a book, or run your first 5k! You don't have to give up the dream of being married, but in the meantime, spend your time making the most of your life.

   a. What can you do, moving forward, to reach new goals? Can you or have you created more goals as a single woman? If not, do so now.

3. We all have some baggage from past relationships, and more than likely, that baggage contains a large number of lies we have told ourselves. Think back over your last few relationships and make a list of four lies you told yourself as reasons

the relationships didn't work out. Examples: *He left me because I wasn't thin enough. He said I was too controlling. I wasn't as sexually adventurous as he wanted me to be.*

a. Now, take each lie you've listed and speak God's truth instead. Examples: *My weight has nothing to do with my worth and beauty. His loss! I have every right to speak my mind and place boundaries in my life. That is not controlling; that's healthy! My future husband will respect my heart, my personal boundaries, and my body.*

8

The Rejection Blessing

"What he opens no one can shut,
and what he shuts no one can open."
(Revelation 3:7 NIV)

No one likes rejection. When it comes to rejection in relationships, we've all been there. It's the type of phrase that comes via phone call, text, or talk: "I think it is best if we are just friends," or "This is not working for me anymore." Or "I've met someone else." Those words can stab the heart, leaving an open wound to mend. Many call it "being dumped." If we are the dumper instead of the dumpee, it doesn't hurt that much; however, when we are the ones rejected, hello heartache and wounded pride!

When a relationship with someone we really loved ends, it can take us months to get over. It hurts because we have to adjust to living solo again while getting the thoughts and memories of the person we loved out of our head. It can also cause us to start questioning ourselves or buy into the belief that something is wrong with us. If we let rejection get the best of us, it may cause us to become depressed with a damaged self-esteem. But Girlfriend, don't go there. No man's rejection is worth becoming depressed over. When someone walks away from your life and no longer wants to be with you, then he wasn't what God wanted for you. If a man walks away, let him—but don't you dare let him take your self-esteem when he leaves.

We serve a God who sees our present and future at the same time, so why is it sometimes hard to have the faith that He will do what He says He will? His Word says that He goes before us and makes the crooked places straight (Isaiah 45:2 NKJV). So when a relationships ends, trust that your Father is keeping you from some crooked paths with that person that He can see but you can't. Or maybe He simply has something way better for you. Does that take the pain away? No, because it is still a loss.

The problem with rejection really escalates when we wrap our life around others and look to them for acceptance and affirmation. All too often we start letting our world revolve around our love. We can often end up building our life around them, and then when the relationship ends, the rejection and loss drive us into an unhealthy and unsafe emotional state because we feel like we have lost our entire identity! This happened to me when I was married the second time. After the divorce, I not only had to adjust as a single mom but I also had to find who I was as a thirty-two-year-old adult.

The steps of a good man are ordered by the LORD.
(PSALM 37:23 NKJV)

Do not let rejection derail you and reroute you into self-doubt and depression. It is God's way of delivering you! Even when it feels like a setback, rejection is God's protection so He can reroute you in another direction. If we want to be all that God has created us to be, then overcoming rejection and its side effects is a must. When people exit our lives, we have to believe that God is allowing it. There will be no room for someone better to enter if the wrong person never exits.

Look back at your past relationships. Can you see now that the relationship's ending was a blessing in disguise? If you can't see that, I promise you will someday. Even if you met the man of your dreams, and you had an amazing relationship that ended in heartbreak, trust that it is for a reason. If it were God's design and purpose for you to be with that person, then you would still be with that person.

A PROMOTION COMMITTEE VERSUS A PURPOSE COMMITTEE

A committee is two or more people working toward a common goal and following a plan. I like to believe that all the people we come in contact with in life and have some level of relationship with can be categorized into two "life committees" when it comes to the plans and goals God has for us. There are people who fit into the "promotion committee": those who are in our lives to teach us something or add temporary value to our lives. Then there are people who fit into the "purpose committee": those who are meant to advance us or help us fulfill our purpose.

Even if you meet a total catch who has a great job, great personality, and several things on your "want list," if he does not share or support the goals you have or the life and the purposes God has created you for, then he is not God's best for you. Don't spend too much time being devastated if a "promotion committee" man walks out of your life. We can learn from all situations. So learn, let go, and know that with each experience we face in life, God can use it to teach us and promote us to the next phase. And ladies, we can't get to the next step if we are still dwelling on and clinging to the last in the past. Believe me when I say that a *promotion man* is nothing compared to the *purpose man.*

Maybe your husband of twenty years cheated on you and you can't see your way through the devastation right now. Grieve and move on because God needed that person to exit your life so He can call forth another plan.

So what do you do when you feel full of disappointment and brokenness? You give it to God. If you have to, close your eyes and picture yourself at His feet, laying your worries and emotions before Him. Your God knows how to heal all things in time; that includes your hurts, feelings of rejection, and emotions.

Yes, rejection hurts. We don't like dealing with loss, because with it comes a life adjustment, a mindset adjustment, and an emotional adjustment. Grief and disappointment are normal, but don't stay stuck in them. Allow yourself to grieve, but keep pressing on and trusting your Father.

CLOSED DOORS ARE A BLESSING

So why does God close doors? There could be one reason or many reasons. Here are a few thoughts, as shared by MJ Blake in her book *Shutting God Out:*

1. God closes doors so that you can change directions.

Many times you keep on doing what you do all your life. But God might certainly have better things in store for you. Since you are comfortable doing what you are now doing and good at it, you will never think about changing directions at all. You will never even give it a passing thought. So to get your attention, God will close doors.

2. God closes doors so that you can learn to pray more.

Closed doors teach you to pray more. They grip your heart with such force that you pray like you've never prayed before. And when doors open, you will thankfully realize that you have moved up another level in the prayer ladder. Therefore pray with all your might when doors close on you.

3. God closes doors so that you will stop trusting in man.

It is only when you have knocked at closed doors that you understand that the help of man cannot be trusted. It is during such times you come to know the true character of those whom you expected would help.

4. God closes doors so that you will wait for His time.

You have to know that there are many reasons why God would do this. He does it to prepare circumstances. He prepares them in such a fashion that it will be to your best advantage when His time comes. If you act before His time, it will be like plucking an unripe fruit. He knows when it is going to be ripe and ready to be eaten. He closes doors so that you will not pluck the unripe fruit. He will open them only when it is ripe. Then it will be to your best advantage.

5. God is preparing you for the task ahead while you wait behind closed doors.

All the waiting, all the hardships and all the misunderstanding and ridicule that you are facing now is building muscles of steely faith in your mind. You are being molded and shaped by God to meet your glorious destiny. The tougher your closed door, the greater the exaltation God has planned for you.[2]

So as you can see, there are several reasons God closes doors. And all of them are for your ultimate good! You better believe fear and rejection are the most common tools the Devil will use to destroy a person's life and self-worth. Change your perspective of rejection before the Devil uses it to change you!

Don't mourn over rejection. Don't take it personally. Just thank God. Rejoice that God has gone before you and changed your direction before you faced a regrettable lesson.

You have a life outside your situation that is waiting to be embraced. Accept the rejection and walk on while pressing through the hurt. Time heals all wounds, and so does learning to embrace and accept the doors God closes.

Rejection is divine protection!

CHAPTER 8: THE REJECTION BLESSING REFLECTION QUESTIONS:

1. Breaking up is hard to do, especially if we're on the receiving end or if we have a hard time hurting other people's feelings. Looking back on your past, you can probably identify several relationships that ended, and while you didn't understand it at the time, now you see that it was actually a blessing! List past relationships below and the reasons you are now glad it didn't work out.

2. Sometimes we deal with rejection in unhealthy ways. Think about some of the negative ways you've handled loss in the past (examples could be avoiding company, binge eating, drinking, engaging in reckless or unhealthy sexual behavior) and instead, make a list of five healthy ways to handle rejection, should you encounter it in the future. (Examples: going for a run instead of eating a box of donuts, accepting a dinner date with friends instead of sitting home alone, getting a pedicure instead of going out to a bar to look for company, or calling a mentor or church counselor to talk to and pray with.

9
Puzzle Pieces

"I have loved you with an everlasting love;
therefore I have drawn you with lovingkindness."
(JEREMIAH 31:3 NASB)

The dating life gets old, doesn't it? It seems like with every failed experience, we end up collecting more scars that show up as bitterness, shame, or regret. I often felt like I was stuck in an ongoing cycle of dating, loving, and giving of myself, then landing in the mud, only to get back up and clean up just to eventually fall in it again.

We wonder where in the world the good men are and where we can find one. We keep trying to meet people, joining dating websites, and asking our friends to set us up in hopes of finding a good man. Here is the problem: we are trying to unfold a plan God has for us in our own way and own time.

One of the quickest ways to get out of this cycle is to embrace being single as a gift and stop making it your life's mission to find a man. Yes, I know you are sick of hearing people tell you to see your singleness as a gift. You are tired of facing loneliness and tired of everyone who meets you asking the stabbing question, "So, are you dating anyone?"

You probably don't want to see your singlehood as a gift, especially when you feel like it is the wrong status to have, and certainly not your chosen lifestyle. I totally get it. If you have any internal self-talk that is trying to convince you that you should be anywhere else but single, consider the following advice:

1. Stop falling into the pit of self-pity. So what that you are single. This is only a season in your life. Even if this season lasts for years, you are in this season for a reason, and it is not to throw a constant pity party.

2. Believe that this is just a season, and one day when God sees that you are ready, your season will change.

3. Embrace this season as a time to "sharpen yourself" so that you can become more desirable and valuable to the one God has for you.

4. Stop focusing on you. There is a world of need out there. Get your eyes off what you don't have and shift your focus to meeting other people's "don't haves." Find other things to fulfill you, such as service and being a gift to others. Get your focus off being "without." Find a purpose to devote your free time to so you won't have time to focus on how alone you feel. Which by the way is just that: a feeling.

I bet God chuckles at the single women who are stuck in the rut of serial dating, driven so often by loneliness. I imagine that as He watches us go on dates and bask in the arms of players and bozos, He is shaking his head, saying, "Just wait, Honey, because on *this* day of *this* year, he will cross your path. So why are you trying to find someone else? It's all about timing for him and for you, my dear. You both have to be ready. Please find contentment in Me and other things and stop putting yourself through this. It's going to fail every time because this is not the man you have a purpose with." If Jesus sat down across from us in one of those moments of despair when we are crying from Mr. Bozo leaving, I imagine He would shake His head and say, "If you only knew."

THE PUZZLE MASTER

Imagine piecing a puzzle together. In your mind, there is a clear picture being formed and each piece is designed to fit with another. You see the beautiful picture on the box, and you look through the pile of pieces, trying to find the one to fit with what you have already laid down. You know that you can't just pick any piece; trying to *make* a piece fit with another won't work without distorting the overall picture *that has already been designed.*

Now imagine God building the puzzle, and on the box is the picture of your life and purpose. As we live our lives, each event, each lesson, each trial, and each victory is a piece He is fitting together. The Bible says that He formed us and called us in our mother's womb. Before we were even conceived, He had a plan and purpose for us; He knew "the big picture." He is the Puzzle Master. He knows exactly what is needed to fit with the other pieces He has already laid, and He is laying each one to create your life and destiny.

We all have a God-given talent and purpose, and if it is our heart's desire, God has a helpmate (also known as a puzzle piece) already designed to fit in our life puzzle to create the beautiful finished picture. The frustrating thing is that we can't see the finished picture like He does. We just have to wait for Him to keep adding pieces. And so often we get tired of waiting, and in our weariness we end up trying to push the Puzzle Master over and find something on our own to fit with the rest. But since it is not the right fit, it will just distort the picture.

This is where faith comes in and we have to learn to walk in faith. God says in Jeremiah 29:11 that He knows the plans He has for us. He sees the final picture. He is building it. He is fitting the pieces together as you live your life. "They are plans to prosper you . . . to give you hope and a future" (NIV). The future He wants to give you, for you to prosper in, is the big picture "on the puzzle box" that only He can see. You have to trust that the Puzzle Master is fitting your life timeline together piece by piece, and many of those pieces involve your future husband. But God can't make him fit with other puzzle pieces that have not been laid down yet. It is a process! The same is applying to his life too. God is building his puzzle and, eventually, your pictures will merge together just as God designed.

It is hard to wait, especially when we so badly want this puzzle-creating process to speed up. We just have to embrace the process. Keep walking in faith and in hope. The Puzzle Master knows what He is doing. When we try to force our own piece to fit with what He is creating, it only slows down the process!

BEING THE BEST YOU

The same God who has the ability to raise a man from the dead, make it rain for forty days and nights, walk on water, multiply food, heal the blind, and form millions of cells together into a living object, has the power to bring two people together for a purpose. Whether you are a single woman who has never married, a divorced woman, a divorced single mom, or an unwed single mom, take this time as a single woman to focus on you and become the *best you* that God desires.

God knows what you need, ladies! He knows what and who is best for you. I know the season of waiting can be discouraging, but in this time of waiting, begin to focus on what blessings you do have. Look at all the positives in this season of your life, and enjoy them. I am sure there are many benefits you can think of.

When that twinge of longing starts pulling at your heart, refocus your thoughts on all of the positives in your life right now. Singleness is a time when you can seize many opportunities. Become a better you so that when God does bless you with your heart's desire, you will be an awesome two.

If you long for a wonderful and fulfilling relationship, stop panicking and trying to push God out of the Puzzle Master seat of your life. Don't keep dating men that you know are wrong for you just so you are not lonely.

Yes, God designed us for relationships. We need relationships, whether they're friends, family, or intimate. There is nothing wrong with longing for companionship and intimate love. But here is what I learned later in life after being consistently frustrated by bad choices in men—God wants to be in that intimate part of our hearts. He wants to be the front and center of our soul. Even when we finally have the relationship we long for, it won't fulfill us like Jesus can and wants to. He longs to be the lover of our soul. He wants to be our heavenly Husband.

THE LOVE OF A LIFETIME

If you have never experienced an intimate walk with Jesus, let me assure you that nothing else can be more fulfilling. He will never leave you. Even when we are married, our husbands can't meet our soul needs like Jesus can. And God wants us to learn this when we are still single so we don't go into the marriage thinking our husband will complete us and fulfill our every emotional and spiritual need. If you long for a family and the love of a lifetime, when you learn to make Him your everything, He will then bless you with your heart's desire.

So become whole and independent in Christ. Be about the Father's business and get busy focusing on doing for others. There is a world of needs out there. Find a cause to be a part of while you are not "tied down" with marriage responsibilities. When we get our focus on God and being His hands and feet and moving beyond ourselves, He will eventually bring someone to our side if it is His will. I know this because He did this for me and for many other women I've talked with. I'm quite sure you've seen it happen in your own circle of friends and family. So ladies, stop looking for what God knows you need! Instead, focus on what He has for you right now. You'll never know what you're being called to do if you don't listen.

As I became more content in Christ and found my identity in Him, He began to urge me to write a book. I chose to be obedient, even though as a struggling single mom, I could not see a way for it to be published. God blessed my obedience and poured the words into me, ordaining every step of the way for me to publish it three and a half years later. A month after starting the book, a writers' class was started for the first time ever at my church, and the doors God opened there were amazing.

That was not a coincidence! I spent many weekend nights alone on my couch, typing, praying, and being with Jesus, and I was content! Did I still have moments of loneliness and frustration? Absolutely. Did I still want to crawl in a hole and disappear to escape the hardships of being a single mom? Most certainly. But, I did not allow my mind and thinking to stay stuck in a negative pit of self-pity. I self-talked myself right out of the pit. I did not let my mind choose its own focus. I chose and forced what my mind focused on.

So where is your focus? Do you need to adjust it? Is your focus on your own life and being sad about what you don't have? If so, you have to choose to change it. You tell your mind what to think. And sometimes a small shift in your mindset is all it takes to help you see the bigger picture—that you are valuable, loved, and worthy of blessings. Having a solid mindset can also provide the strength and confidence you need to avoid settling for less than you want and deserve.

CHAPTER 9: PUZZLE PIECES
REFLECTION QUESTIONS:

1. Imagine your life as one big puzzle. You might see all the pieces before you and still feel that a few are missing. *Husband. Baby. Goal weight. Successful career. Dream house.* God says in Jeremiah 29:11 that He knows the plans He has for us. He sees the final picture. List your missing puzzle pieces below and then give each one to God, telling Him your desire, and trusting that He hears your heart.

2. In this time of life, focus on being the strong woman that you want to be! Below, list five benefits in your own life of being single right now.

3. What's your vision? If you've never created a vision board, now is a perfect time to do so! (Google "vision board" for endless ideas.) Vision boards take many forms, and they are visual reminders of goals we set for ourselves. Spend some time over the next week looking through Pinterest, magazines, and other resources to gather images and words that represent the life you want to live. Then once you've created your board, place it where you will see it every day and be reminded of your bright future! Remember if God calls you to do something, He will line up the ability and make a way.

10

The Dangers of Settling

Let us not become weary in doing good,
for at the proper time we will reap a harvest
if we do not give up.
(GALATIANS 6:9 NIV)

My gorgeous dancer friend, Shauna, will tell you now that she was totally aware she was settling in the past, and she deeply regrets how she allowed fear to make her stay in a bad situation. She ignored the still, small feeling that it wasn't right.

A year after a failed marriage with a man who cheated on her, and when her son was three, she met another man and fell in love. When the two-year relationship ended, she sat on my couch in tears, saying, "I don't know why I stayed with him. I saw so many things wrong, but I stayed because I thought he loved me. I didn't think I would find anyone else who would want a single mom with a young child."

At thirty-four, Shauna is still single and is now expecting another child with that man who told her for two years that he would always be there for her. So where is he now? With another woman he was also secretly dating while he was with her. She had no idea. She is now left to pick up the pieces of her broken and abandoned heart while finding the strength to face being a single mom of two.

There are stories after stories of women who have stayed in bad relationships even when they knew the relationships were not God's best for them. There were red flags, a lack of peace, or others saying, "Girl, you need to run!" We have all ignored the caution signs God and others were flashing in front of our faces, only to end up with hindsight kicking us in the rear end. Some of you are lucky you can walk away from mistakes with only a broken heart and hard lessons learned. Others are left with consequences or great loss that they will carry for a long time.

We can all look back at our past and realize we settled big time at one point or another. But, the best thing about mistakes (and sometimes the only good thing) is that they mold us if we allow them to. It may have hurt like there is no tomorrow when they ended, but we are stronger and wiser now. So count it all joy! Thank God for the yesterdays and for all the mistakes, because if mistakes are viewed the right way, they can be seen as something that made you even more marvelous.

WHAT MAKES US SETTLE?

We all have ideals, standards, goals, dreams, and a "want list," but somewhere in the frustrating journey of life, we end up making a directional move that we know is less than what we have really wanted. Why do we do this? For one or multiple reasons: Because it seemed like a good opportunity at the time, because there was nothing else better coming along, or because we got tired of the way life was and discontentment drove us to it.

Maybe there is a void in us and dating makes us feel better about who we are, or we settle because we doubt that we can do better, or maybe our faith grows weary and we start to doubt that God will bring something better our way. Or maybe we get tired of waiting, period. Regardless, the drive to thrive on less than what we really want for ourselves is *settling*. And settling should never be an accepted standard.

"The minute you settle for less than you deserve,
you get even less than you settled for."
—MAUREEN DOWD

When it comes to relationships, settling often seems much more desirable than the alternative—being alone. Some people settle so they will have companionship, or for financial reasons, or for personal or familial security. But regardless of the reason, settling can often hurt both your heart and the relationship. Our settling can also hurt the lives of those we love and who love us.

So what is the answer? Learn to be content while you wait, no matter how long that may be. If you do date, be extremely cautious and have your head on straight. Take the time to build a solid friendship, which will give you the time you need to learn the person's character.

A DEVIOUS PLAN PLANTED BY OUR ENEMY

I've mentioned it before but I'll say it again—the Lord created you with a plan and purpose in mind. You were fearfully and wonderfully made for a purpose. Psalm 139:13 says, "For you created my inmost being; you knit me together in my mother's womb" (NIV). Often it takes us many years of trials and "life" training before His purpose is revealed. And it is not just one event or one mission that He has for us to do. He has given us many abilities to serve multiple purposes in different seasons of life. He has a destiny for each of us, but it does not always mean it will culminate in one big event or one specific ministry.

We can be His hands and feet in many aspects and seasons of our lives. But how healthy, stable, happy, and effective are you going to be if you are stuck in a bad relationship that you settled for? We can avoid many heartaches and consequences if we are strong enough to avoid settling.

After I made a U-turn in following my will and own ways, to the road called "His Ways," God began to show me how He sees me. He began to remind me of His unfailing, non-condemning love. I began to reclaim my vision and find my identity in Him, and I started seeing myself differently. I began to believe that I can "do all things (and be all things) through Christ who gives me strength" (Philippians 4:13). That included getting through lonely times and facing discouragement after every proposal I heard about, engagement party, wedding, and baby shower I attended, and romance movie I saw. I actually talked to myself in the mirror a few times: "Girl, you've got to quit moping and move on with yourself!" Yes, I pep talked myself out loud because in those alone times no one else was speaking, so I spoke to Jesus and myself. So if it helps, there is no shame in verbally pep talking yourself!

THE FORCES AGAINST YOU

As you begin to make a shift in your life and let go of things that have kept you down—be it your wounded heart, your negative self-view, unforgiveness that you have held on to, or just a "poisonous" person period—you need to expect that Satan will be mad. Do you think he wants us to grow in Christ? Absolutely not, so he will throw things at us to pull us down and steal the joy and personal growth God is building in us. John 10:10 says, "The thief comes only to steal and kill and destroy" (NIV). How can the enemy steal from us?

1. By bringing distractions into our lives that shift our focus and rob our time.
2. By bringing people into our life (wrong men) that appear to be good for us, but they bring defeat and lead us down the wrong "path."
3. By killing our spirit and minds with damaged emotions that keep us locked in a self-torture chamber.
4. Through life challenges that start to drain the joy and faith right out of us.

In the life of every Christian, here are ten things the Devil targets and determines to rob us of. These have been adapted from a message preached by Pastor Kehinde Adegbolahan:[3]

1. **Purpose**: It is purpose that gives a life definition and mean-

ing. A life with no purpose becomes worthless.

2. **Desire**: The Bible says the desires of our hearts shall be granted (when our minds are set on Him), but when desires are killed, frustration sets in.

3. **Vision**: Vision takes a person to their destination. Vision creates room for the next level and enlarges our territory. It drives us to rise to a different place in life. When vision is lost through trials and heartache, stagnancy prevails.

4. **Gifts**: The Word of God says, "A man's gift makes room for him and brings him before great men" (Proverbs 18:16 NASB). Many have not been able to stand in their purpose and dreams because the gifts that would open doors have been buried.

5. **Calling**: As the kingdom of God threatens the kingdom of darkness running rampant on earth, the Devil does not want anyone to fulfill their purpose for God. The fulfillment of your purpose means the defeat of the Devil's kingdom.

6. **Potential**: Potential is defined as what you can do but have not done. The Devil prefers it when men and women do not wake up to their own potentials. Self-doubt of what you can do through Christ—who gives us strength and pours out an anointing—leads to an unfulfilled life.

7. **Expectation**: The expectation of many has been killed due to lack of faith. When you are not expectant, you end up receiving nothing.

8. **Voice**: Every man has been given a voice by God. One of the joys of the enemy is to silence voices and make sure the authority of your voice is lost.

9. **Effectiveness**: When you get stuck in the rut of the aftermath of bad choices (settling), your focus can often change because you are left having to rebuild or climb out of the rut. This can cause you to temporarily lose effectiveness.

10. **Life**: This represents your divine assignment in life. It's the Devil's delight when men and women do not discover, start, or complete the agenda of God for their lives.

When we settle, especially in the area of men and intimate

relationships, it can eventually wreak havoc on our life, which is ultimately a distraction and causes a weapon the enemy formed against us to prosper. When the Lord wants to promote you to your purpose in life, He will bring the right people across your path to bless you and walk with you or help accelerate you. When the enemy wants to demote you, he will bring people across your path that will cause you to lose your focus and effectiveness and may inflict great pain upon your life.

Now, you may think this is bad news, but there is no perfect man out there. There is no perfect relationship, and no matter how wonderful the man may be, all relationships have their ups and downs and take work. We all have flaws and issues. But you can't ignore big red flags or forgo what is most important to you just so you can "have someone" to avoid loneliness. Don't overlook big flaws thinking that things will change or get better in time. And don't settle for less than your spiritual equal. Especially don't ignore a gut feeling the Holy Spirit gives you that something just isn't right, that it's not God's best. If there is a bad gut feeling in you at some point in the relationship, don't toss it up as your own fears. It is the Holy Spirit warning you because God sees your future and knows what lies ahead and that that relationship is not part of His plan for you. As hard as it is to walk away, there may be something He wants to spare you from before you get more deeply involved or say "I do."

VALUE YOURSELF TOO MUCH TO SETTLE

People settle when it comes to relationships and stay stuck in bad relationships for several reasons.

1. We get tired of being alone and single and/or bored.
2. We fear that no one else better will come along.
3. We want more financial stability.
4. We think we can change him or the situation.
5. We tell ourselves that God has the power to change anything, and if we have faith He will. (Although He is powerful and does change people, that does not mean you are meant to be with the man and that He will change him for

you.)

6. We crave sex and affection and we want the emotional safety of one sex partner.
7. And harsh but often true . . . we are addicted to the drama.

Settling is like going shoe shopping for a pair of heels to go with a certain dress you bought for an event. When you find just the right-looking pair on sale, you buy them even if they do not feel totally comfortable, because after all, they are the right price and look super. You feel glamorous and beautiful, but after a few hours, you are flat-out uncomfortable and you just want to take them off. To avoid being different you continue your evening with poise, determined to deal with the pain. Then when the event is over, you sit in your misery while nursing multiple blisters, and the thought that ran through your mind several times during the event hits you again: *I wish I would have kept looking for something else. I made a horrible choice and now I hurt!*

Take it from someone who settled multiple times out of fear of being alone and who spent twelve years lost and broken because of it. The moment you start to settle for less than what God wants for you is the moment you invite the enemy in to begin to disrupt the plan God wants for you. When you settle, you send your own self down a road called "Detour." *Avoid the detours at all costs because detours only bring delays!*

Here are some reasons why you should never settle for less than what you want:

1. It isn't fair to you!

When you settle for less than what you want, you are not valuing yourself—you are selling yourself short. Don't value yourself at less than your God-given worth.

2. It's not fair to the other person.

Think about how you would feel if you knew your significant other was settling for you. Nobody wants to feel like the backup plan!

3. You will be unavailable when the right person comes along.

Don't tell yourself you will date this person until "Mr. Right finds you." Starting a relationship with Mr. Right when you are directly coming out of a previous one can be messy—the previous relationship can do serious damage even if you never intended to get too close. Then when Mr. Wonderful comes along, you are not "all together" and emotionally healthy.

Love and value yourself too much to settle. Have enough belief in yourself and in God that in time you will meet what your heart desires because God wants you to have it! He will bring the right man that is in His plan.

Don't let loneliness, or the thoughts of never finding anyone better, cause you to settle. You cannot see your future and what God has in store for you.

I thank God that I did not continue my cycle of settling to avoid being alone, or I would have missed an amazing blessing He had in store. I am so thankful I learned to find contentment and a strong identity in Him. Had I not, I would have missed something even better than I had ever asked for. And that very same kind of wonderful could be in your future too!

CHAPTER 10: THE DANGERS OF SETTLING REFLECTION QUESTIONS:

1. When we see red flags, we shouldn't ignore them! But you must first know what your non-negotiables are in order to spot them. Below, make a list of up to five "red-flag" issues that you will not accept in relationships.

2. Now that you have your non-negotiables, make a list of up to five qualities on your "must have" list. The next time you meet a potential match, measure them against your lists as you get to know them and act accordingly!

Section Three:
Redefining Your
Journey to Healing

"Come to me, all you who are weary and burdened, and I will give you rest. Take my yoke upon you and learn from me, for I am gentle and humble in heart, and you will find rest for your souls. For my yoke is easy and my burden is light."
(MATTHEW 11:28–30 NIV)

11

Forgiving Yourself and Others

Create in me a clean heart, O God, and put a new and right spirit within me. Do not cast me away from your presence, and do not take your holy spirit from me. Restore to me the joy of your salvation, and sustain in me a willing spirit.
(PSALM 51:10–12 NRSV)

Unforgiveness is an inner battle that can ruin many areas of your life and hinder your relationship with Christ and other people. It takes less energy to forgive someone and see them through the eyes of Christ than it does to stay angry and hold a grudge.

But he broke my heart . . .
He cheated on me . . .
He abused me . . .
He used me . . .
He damaged my self-esteem . . .
He betrayed me time and time again . . .
He stole from me . . .

The list of wrongs can be a mile long. People hurt us and leave wounds. Most people in life are walking around and existing in a state of brokenness, immorality, selfishness, emotional turmoil from damaged emotions, warped thinking, addictions, or just locked in some form of bondage from a stronghold placed by the enemy. And in that state of being, they hurt themselves and others. Yes, we've all been hurt and even hurt someone else with our words or actions. But the key to peace is forgiveness.

OVERCOMING RESENTMENT

Forgiving someone is hard, especially if it is someone who altered our life by their actions. It requires an act of total self-surrender and a mindset of letting go of the need for revenge, as well as the release of negative thoughts of bitterness. That is often the hardest part—releasing the negative thoughts and reminders. It sometimes has to happen daily or even hourly!

It is easy to *say* we forgive someone, but so many times our words do not match the lingering mental state that can hold our mind hostage. This lingering state of mind is called resentment. And behind this name come bitter statements such as: *How could they? Do they know what they did to me? They ruined my life! They robbed me of my youth! They destroyed my dreams and who I was! They messed up my world. They left me in despair. I wish someone would hurt them the way they hurt me.* The list goes on and on.

Forgiving someone who has done us wrong and deeply wounded us is one of the hardest things to conquer in life, but if we don't make the decision to do it, the negative emotions rooted in unforgiveness will eventually alter our lives. How do I know this? Because it is one of the games the enemy plays with our minds and lives. It is one of those strongholds he loves to see us stuck in. When we can't get beyond the resentment toward someone else for hurting us, the Devil will take that and plant ongoing reminders that mess with our minds and keep us from living in the peace and freedom that Christ has for us.

It took me a long time to get over what the con man did to me. Every time the thought of him came to mind, a knot churned in my stomach. The anger I had toward him fueled resentment, but what I finally realized was that *I was angrier at myself* for being so vulnerable and naive and allowing him to do what he did to me. I felt so much shame that I had stayed with him when the Holy Spirit had warned me. I settled for him and was so snowed over by his love and promises that they blinded me. I felt so ashamed that I had sacrificed some of my "strong roots" and backed down on some of my beliefs that had molded me. I tried to fit his mold of what he wanted and needed. And in the process, my own mold was cracked.

How often have you done that? How often have you changed yourself to be more of what you think a man desires? It is not uncommon. But let me tell you, when it is the man God has for you, you will be respected and admired for just who God designed you to be.

Looking back now at the last thirteen years of my life, I wish I would have taken time, after that traumatic event that left me so hurt and wounded, to heal and find myself in Christ and become a confident strong woman at a young age. My life would look so different now had I done that, but I didn't. I just kept masking my hurt, insecurities, and self-pity in the arms of another man. I kept icing my scars until they were numb with other relationships. I can clearly see now, more than a decade later, that I was filling my emptiness with validation and the security of a man and not with Christ. I can see now that all I was doing was adding more wounds on top of existing ones. Luckily, I finally took that time years later after several more mistakes and many more situations that required forgiveness and healing.

Even though time healed my wounds from the con man experience and my life went on, I didn't stop resenting him until I finally went on a journey with Christ to find myself in Him. I will never forget the day I was writing in my journal and God revealed something to me.

In my spirit I was reminded that we hurt Christ time and time again, but He never harbors resentment or even holds on to our wrongs. God reminded me that I had no right to withhold forgiveness from John, because my lack of forgiveness was holding me back from becoming what He desired for me. And then God reminded me of the words He said when hanging on the cross: "Forgive them, for they know not what they do." That became a phrase I clung to. "Amy, forgive him, for he knew not what he did through his own personal brokenness." As I began to say that over and over again with tears running down my face, my resentment was slowly replaced with grace. It became easier for me to release resentment toward him because I knew he was lost in a world of sin and bondage, and he hurt me in the process of being messed up and lost in it.

People come from all walks of life and are at all different maturity levels. Most people in life, especially unbelievers, are walking around housing past hurts, unforgiveness, sorrow, and anger. Some people are just plain messed up on the inside and mask it well because they don't know how to find healing on their own or through Christ. When someone hurts you or acts in a way that damages you somehow, it is so much easier not to harbor negative thought toward them when we have this mindset: "Father, forgive them and help me forgive them because they know not what they do in their own state of damaged emotions and selfishness."

NO, IT'S NOT FAIR

"It's not fair! They don't deserve forgiveness." Have you said this before too?

How can we forgive someone who forever altered our life and tainted and forever scarred what we once saw as something beautiful? How does a mom forgive the man who abducted and murdered her child? How does the young girl forgive someone who raped her and took her virginity? How does the woman forgive the man who beat her and destroyed her self-worth? How does the young woman forgive a man who abused her and destroyed her self-esteem in a toxic relationship? Sometimes we don't want to forgive, and our emotions and hatred are so enormous that we simply feel we can't. We may also feel that the person who hurt us *doesn't deserve forgiveness*. But here is where the stronghold is: even if they don't deserve forgiveness, not forgiving only gives them the power to continue to hurt you! They can be long gone and living a new life without a thought or care of you. By continuing to hold on to bitterness or resentment, they are still affecting you!

Moving beyond the feelings provoked by memories is a task that requires a great deal of mental discipline. Some wonder how it is even possible. To be real, *forgiveness isn't fair,* but God commands us to forgive because He paid the ultimate price for forgiveness when we didn't ask for it or deserve it. Instead of walking to the cross with a "How could they?" mentality, He hung in agony while He said the words, "Father, forgive them, for they know not what they do." Because He did it for us, I know He wants us to extend grace to others.

God also knows what unforgiveness and bitterness can to do to us mentally and physically. If we can look at unforgiveness as what it truly is—a dark pit that Satan wants us to fall into and trap us in—perhaps a desperation will be created in us. A desperation to let go of the mental memories that stab at our emotions.

Picture something in your mind as you read this next paragraph: In a beautiful backyard there is a large, stately tree with a wide trunk. God designed this tree to be strong and serve a purpose in the forest that is now a backyard. Around the base of the tree are grass and flowers; it's a beautiful, manicured site. Now fast-forward ten years. Over time, as the tree has grown, the roots have begun to protrude from the ground and bust up the yard, flowers, and grass that once surrounded it. The tree itself is still beautiful, but the ground around it is now destroyed into a crumbled mess of dirt and grass. Although that tree remains a stately sight and still functions with purpose, the foundation around it is broken up and no longer reflects what it once did.

Unforgiveness, which settles in our spirits as resentment or bitterness, is like those tree roots. If it grows and remains in us, it will eventually affect the "foundation" we stand on and crumble everything around us. As I mentioned before, bitterness and unforgiveness are strongholds from the enemy. They hold our minds and souls captive with tormenting memories and feelings that can eventually make our souls and even body sick.

KEEPING A RECORD OF WRONGS

I have an acquaintance who went through a horrible divorce

in her thirties. Her husband cheated on her and abandoned her and their two children, and he fled to another state with his mistress. Not only did she deal with her own hurt and anger but also her kids' emotions. She loathed her ex-husband and never forgave him. She was overtaken with resentment for many years as she had to face each day as a single mom, and faced many hardships.

Even though she remarried later when her children were in college, she never let go of the anger and bitterness she had toward her first husband. And what she did not realize until later on was that over the years, she had kept a record of wrongs of every person who had hurt her in some way in her life. In her older age, she developed severe chronic arthritic pain. The doctors could never find a cause for it. It is my belief, along with that of many psychologists, that bitterness and unresolved anger can be the root of psychosomatic illnesses. Unforgiveness stays in your body and can be like a cancer that slowly eats at your soul.

GIVING A GIFT TO YOURSELF

Forgiveness is not for the other person; *it is for you*. When you choose to forgive, you are releasing yourself from a mental prison that you could potentially remain in for years. God knows sin blinds us. God knows that we deal with a spirit world that seeks to captivate our minds, our actions, and our souls. That is why He said in 2 Corinthians 10:4, "The weapons we fight with are not the weapons of the world . . . they have divine power to demolish strongholds" (NIV).

As I mentioned before, resentment can be a stronghold! Bitterness and resentment contradict peace. We can't be walking around full of godly confidence and joy while holding a grudge coupled with gnawing resentment.

If you feel resentment toward someone who has hurt you, mentally lay it down and ask God to take it from you. Begin to say the prayer of Jesus on the cross. "Father, forgive (say their name), because he knows not what he did/does." If you are also having a hard time forgiving yourself, put your name in that prayer.

I had to get to a place in my life where I took all the anger and resentment, the memories that constantly fueled self-pity, and the anger that I had at myself, and get before God and ask Him to take them from me and cover me and all the resentment inside me with His blood. I had to get to a place where I finally stopped feeling ashamed of my past and all the stupid mistakes I had made, even when I knew better. Before the resentment destroyed me, I poured out my heart to God, wrote down all the things that I was angry about and holding on to, and laid them down at my mental altar and asked God to take them from me. I forced myself to have a different mindset. Even in my present life, I have to continuously forgive my ex-husband for actions he makes. It is not easy, but I know I have to do it.

My past is my past. I can't change it, but I can learn from it. I can't continue to let people who hurt me in the past affect my present or my future. Even if they are people I still have to see in my present, I choose to see them as Christ does and not as someone who did (or does) me wrong and hurt me. This is very difficult, especially when the person throws hurtful challenges at you on a continual basis. But what are the choices? Forgive and be at peace and free or continue to let the person who hurts you have power over you.

I choose freedom.

HOW CAN I FORGIVE?[4]

1. Acknowledge your own inner pain.

You have the right to hurt, but acknowledge how holding on to the hurt may be affecting your present mental state. As much as you want to, you can't change what has been done. So the only choice you have is to allow yourself to hurt from it. Begin to process the hurt and as you do so, realize that *dwelling* on it or being bitter will only keep you from becoming a healthier person.

2. Try to understand the point of view and motivations of the person to be forgiven; replace anger with compassion.

There are so many people who carry pain and bondage with them through life, and they live out and act through those emotions. Because of this, they may lack the proper ability to treat others right. All people mentally, emotionally, and spiritually mature at different rates. And some people just simply can't get beyond their own selves to be able to think or comprehend how they hurt and affect others. We live in a broken world full of broken people.

Even if you believe the person who hurt you knew exactly what they were doing, you still have to understand that they may have been driven by or operating through deep wounds that you have no perception of. Let me say it again: as long as you are filled with bitterness and resentment toward people who hurt you, all you are doing is continuing to give them the power to damage you. And if you don't let go of it, you will carry it into your next relationship.

Release yourself from a mental prison that bitterness keeps you locked in. Make the choice to walk in emotional freedom!

3. Forgive yourself for your role in the relationship.

Perform the overt act of forgiveness verbally or in writing, both to yourself and to the other person, expressing all of your feelings and explaining why you need to let go. If the person is dead, unreachable, or someone you want any contact with in the future, you can still write down your feelings in letter form and choose to keep it, throw it away, tear it into tiny pieces, or burn it as a symbol of letting go. You don't need to mail that letter—it is therapeutic just to write it all down.

You may want to take the letter to a counselor and talk about it. You can also write down all of your excess "baggage" on a piece of paper and discard it in whatever manner feels best to you, when you are ready to really let go.

WHAT FORGIVENESS IS NOT . . .[5]

- Forgiveness is not forgetting or pretending it didn't happen. It did happen, and we need to retain the lesson learned without holding on to the pain.
- Forgiveness is not excusing. We excuse a person who is not to blame. We forgive because a wrong was committed.

- Forgiveness is not giving permission to continue hurtful behaviors, nor is it condoning the behavior in the past or in the future.
- Forgiveness is not reconciliation. We have to make a separate decision about whether to reconcile with the person we are forgiving or whether to maintain our distance.

Forgiveness is not a one-time act. We may get to a place where we feel liberated from going through a period of healing and true forgiveness, but in time, resentment tries to attach its ugly claws on our minds again. Learn to forgive daily if it is required, and ask the Lord to help you see the person who wronged you through eyes of grace like He does.

You may even try to pray out loud. Say, "In the name of Jesus, I chose to forgive. I come against you, spirit of resentment. The Lord binds you from placing a stronghold on me. I have forgiven (say their name), and I will continue to have a heart of forgiveness."

Wounds can run deep. Keep forgiving them until the Spirit of Christ is flowing though you and can replace the hurt with a Christ-like compassion. That is what forgiveness really is. It is letting go of our own self-damaged emotions and replacing them with compassion. I know this is easier said than done, but stop giving power to someone who hurt you in the past (or recently) to continue to hurt you. Unforgiveness is self-inflicted turmoil.

Free yourself from a prison of resentment. Walk in peace, Sister. Forgive freely!

CHAPTER 11: FORGIVING YOURSELF AND OTHERS REFLECTION QUESTIONS:

1. Unforgiveness is an inner battle that must be won to have a fruitful life. Below, list any people who still stir feelings of resentment or anger within you.

2. Now look at each name, understanding that this person likely has no idea how much hurt they caused you. While you cannot make someone apologize, you can release your own grudge against them.

3. When you are ready, hold each name in your mind and forgive them, knowing that this benefits you more than them. Say, "In the name of Jesus, I choose to forgive (their name). I come against you, spirit of resentment; the Lord binds you from placing a stronghold on me. I have forgiven (their name) and I will continue to have a heart of forgiveness." You deserve to be free from the chains of negativity that hold you back. Forgive and set yourself free!

4. Speaking of setting yourself free, you might also benefit from forgiving yourself. We don't like to acknowledge it, but self-forgiveness can be a compassionate gift we give ourselves for any actions or decisions in our past that still haunt us. As you think about each instance, take a deep breath, ask God to forgive you (which He does instantly), and then say, "I forgive myself for (the action/decision). I love myself and choose to live in grace."

12
Aligning Your Mind

*"You will forget your misery; you will remember it
as waters that have passed away."*
(JOB 11:16 ESV)

If you want to move forward in your life and have victory as a woman who is strong and emotionally whole and healthy, get your thought life in order and under control. So often negative thoughts about who or how we are bombard our minds. And thoughts are just thoughts; they are not always true or relevant. Most of the time, they are thoughts planted by the enemy. We have to get to a place in life where we tell ourselves, "I can, I am, and I will!" way more than we ever tell ourselves, "I can't, I won't, and I'm not."

No matter what we face in life, be it a bad breakup, abuse, rejection, death of a spouse, or facing each day with infirmities, we will have a conscious and subconscious thought process about ourselves and our situations going through our minds. You have heard that saying "You are what you eat," right? Well, the same applies to your thoughts. You are what you think. The mind is the powerhouse and control center of our body. It is what tells everything else what to do. So if we are telling ourselves that we are failures, or not pretty or not good enough, we will eventually begin to operate within that realm of negativity and it will start to affect other areas of our lives. Our self-esteem and self-image may be the greatest areas impacted when we continue to buy into the negative thoughts the enemy torments us with. Don't believe the thoughts that totally contradict the Word of God.

TAKE YOUR THOUGHTS CAPTIVE

When I was thirty-six, I looked back on all the relationship mistakes I had made and the life that I had established. I was mad at myself and had put myself on God's damaged-goods list. Yes, of course, it was a list I created, but I allowed myself to believe that God was disappointed in me. Was that true? Of course not, but I had listened to the negative self-talk way too long. Satan had won the battle in my mind, and I believed the label I gave myself of "messed-up, damaged failure."

After reading some books on the subject of the mind and our thought process, God quickly showed me that I needed to align my thinking with the Word and learn to take my thoughts captive before they took me captive—and they were already doing a great job of that. It wasn't easy to do. I had to make a conscious daily effort to change my thought patterns, speak Scripture to my situations, and learn to view myself the way God does. And let me tell you: I have not conquered and arrived yet. It is something I still practice daily. As long as we are on this earth, we will battle with the enemy. His quickest and easiest battle strategy is to attack the mind. And you have to learn to fight your enemy or you will become a defeated Christian instead of the victorious conqueror that Christ says you are!

Our minds are bombarded with thousands of thoughts a day. If we want to have a successful and mentally healthy life, we have to learn how to filter our thoughts and determine what is actually true, what is from our emotions, and what is from the enemy. Our minds can be our worst hindrance or the greatest tool we have. But understand this: just like you make your hands and feet do deliberate actions by purposeful thinking, so you also have to control your mind with focused intention.

Take a moment to read several Scriptures God put in His instruction manual about our thoughts and our minds. (I've added the emphasis on certain phrases.)

Romans 12:2 NIV: "Do not conform to the pattern of this world, but be transformed by the *renewing of your mind.* Then you will be able to test and approve what God's will is—his good, pleasing and perfect will."

Isaiah 26:3 NIV: "You will keep in perfect peace those whose *minds are steadfast,* because they trust in you."

Romans 8:6 NIV: "The mind governed by the flesh is death, but *the mind governed by the Spirit is life and peace.*"

Ephesians 4:22–24 NIV: "You were taught, with regard to your former way of life, to put off your old self, which is being corrupted by its deceitful desires; to *be made new in the attitude of your minds.*"

Colossians 3:2 NIV: "*Set your minds* on things above, not on earthly things."

1 Peter 5:8 NIV: "*Be alert and of sober mind.* Your enemy the devil prowls around like a roaring lion looking for someone to devour."

All of these Scriptures require deliberate action: set our minds, make our attitudes new, renew our minds, govern our minds, make our minds steadfast. In a nutshell, you have to tell your mind what to do and choose your beliefs and what to focus on. Be the commander-in-chief of the battle in your mind, because if you aren't, your mind and thoughts will begin to command you.

As single people we can easily listen to and be affected by many thoughts that bombard us, such as: *Why am I still single? There must be something wrong with me. There are so few good people left, so I better take what I can get. I am a reject and no one wants me. I am so tired of being lonely and I have needs, so why not? I am going to grow old alone. No one will want a mom with kids. I am a failure and people must see me that way.*

The negative list goes on and on. Don't let these types of thoughts fill your mind, and certainly don't believe them! Do not put a label on yourself and believe and operate through thoughts that are contradicting the Word of God and what He says regarding you.

OUR MINDS ARE POWERFUL

Who made our brains? God did. So wouldn't you imagine that the Creator of our minds knows how they operate? Why would God put these verses in His Word for the entire world to read for generations? Because He knows how our minds affect our body, life, and actions. Proverbs 23:7 says, "For as he thinks in his heart, so is he" (NKJV). What you think on, you operate on and eventually become.

In other words, what controls your mind controls your life. Our minds control our actions, behaviors, moods, and emotions.

Think about this for a moment: Where does loneliness come from? Our thoughts. Where is depression generated? In our thoughts (apart from chemical imbalances).

Where does anger come from? Our thoughts.

Where does low self-esteem come from? Our thoughts.

Where does anxiety come from? Our thoughts.

Where does resentment come from? Our thoughts.

Where does fear come from? Our thoughts.

I could go on and on, but I think you get the point. You may point out that depression and anxiety and fear can be physical feelings and come from chemical imbalances. That is very true, but where do some physical feelings come from, such as stress and anxiety? They can stem from what our mind is dwelling on—our thoughts!

The number-one way we are attacked by the enemy is through our mind, our thought process. We have constant self-talk throughout the day, and the enemy tries to come in and haunt our minds with negative self-talk. Our minds control everything we do, and we become vulnerable to strongholds being placed in our minds when we do not learn to take our thoughts captive and submit them to the Word of God. We have to learn to control our thoughts before they control us.

First Peter 5:8 says to "be alert and of sober (awake and aware) mind." Awake to what, you may be asking? You have to be awake and alert to the battle created by the enemy to devour you—to devour your mind, which affects every area of life. Do not let your mind be bombarded with negative self-talk such as: *I am worthless. He dumped me because I am flawed. I will never have someone love me. This pain is too great. I am never going to get beyond this. My life is over.* That is what Joyce Meyers calls "stinking thinking," and that kind of thinking will force you into a pit.

We are in a daily war zone. We do not war against flesh and blood on a daily basis. Our war is against the powers of this dark world and against the spiritual forces of evil (Ephesians 6:12). So, every day we must wake up, put on our soldier armor, and stand guard. We have to be responsible to guard what we *allow* to come into our minds and also be responsible to take some things *out* of our minds.

No one can force you to think a certain way. No one else can change your thoughts either. The only one who can control your mind is you. No one can be responsible for your internal thoughts but you. In the same sense that you have to take care of your health and watch what you eat, you have to manage the thoughts in your mind and watch what you allow yourself to think. This is hard, but it can be done with deliberate effort.

THE SCIENCE OF THINKING

God ordained this Scripture in His Word thousands of years ago before science and technology existed. As brain-imaging technology has advanced, so has our understanding of how the brain works. In the last ten years, we have learned so much about the brain due to brain scans. One amazing discovery is that our brain doesn't stop growing when our body does; that is, it has the ability to adapt and change right up to the end of our life.

If you like to research and learn new information, look up the science and studies of neuroplasticity. It refers to changes in neural pathways and synapses, which are due to changes in behavior, environment, and neural processes. It revolves around the concept and proven studies that our thoughts can change the structure and function of our brains. Neuroplasticity research now proves what many have long known: that you can rewire your brain to think and act in ways that lead to greater success in work, love, and health.[6]

Rewiring your brain will not happen overnight. It takes repetition, but it is now proven by science to be possible.

According to research, we have anywhere from 12,000 to 60,000 thoughts per day, but 78 percent of those thoughts are exactly the same as we had the day before. It's called habitual thinking, and most of our habitual thinking is negative.[7] Negative thoughts are particularly draining. Thoughts containing words like "never," "not," and "can't" deplete the body by producing corresponding chemicals that weaken us. No wonder we're worn out at the end of the day! But here is some fabulous news: if you can recognize a negative or unproductive and self-defeating thought, you can consciously choose to change it, and by doing this repetitively, you will start to rewire your brain and your life. Take Pastor Will Bowen, for example.

Pastor Will Bowen of Christ Church Unity in Kansas City knows well the power of changing the way you think. In an effort to help his congregation find a concrete way to focus on what they *do* want rather than what they *don't* want, he created a purple bracelet and gave one to everyone at church one Sunday. Because it often takes at least 21 days to create a new habit, the idea was for people to switch the bracelet to the other wrist if they found themselves complaining (one of the most common forms of negative thinking). They had to keep switching it to the other arm until they'd gone the full 21 days without a single complaint.

The "Complaint-Free World" project exploded from 250 bracelets to five million in nine months. Pastor Will receives letters daily from schools, prisons, hospitals, churches, businesses, even the Pentagon, telling him what a powerful and positive impact the bracelets are having. Families are getting closer. People's health is improving. People are turning their lives around.[8]

The bottom line is this—stop allowing negative thoughts to dictate your moods, or how you act, and what true reality is. Don't tell yourself you won't ever find Mr. Right, ever get over this or that, ever be happy, ever get over being afraid or lonely, ever get over him, or ever stop missing him. Stop with the stinking thinking!

The quality of life you live is determined by the quality of your thoughts toward yourself and the way you operate day to day. So, if you want a quality life, have quality thoughts!

COMBAT YOUR NEGATIVE THOUGHTS WITH GOD'S WORD

For anyone who has ever dealt with stress, worry, or anxiety, you know how tormenting it can be when it grabs hold of our mind and even our bodies. Without taking our minds captive and refusing to "give in" to the tormenting thoughts, we are left vulnerable for torments to latch onto us and eventually become strongholds the enemy places on our life.

True peace, true courage, and true love come from God. The Lord Jesus Christ died for us so that we would be set free from the evil of the world. Nothing can win against the One who conquered death. When we have Christ in us, we have a God-given authority over the Devil. Because Christ has already defeated Satan, he can't do a thing to us but torment us and put strongholds on us if we allow him to. Use the God-given authority you have to speak against him and the attacks he tries to come at you with.

When faced with worry, anxiety, fear, or depression, do these things:

1. Get before God. Believe He is who He says He is, and He will do what He says He can.
2. Realize that not one bit of worry or fear will do you any good. Worrying and stressing about something does not change one bit of the present or future. The only thing it can change is our mood and emotions.
3. Realize that worry and depression are nothing more than

the enemy tormenting your mind and trying to hold it hostage.

4. Make a list of the Scriptures that combat your thinking. The minute that your stinking thinking starts, combat it with the Word. Declare the Word over your worry, doubt, and fear.

AS SOLDIERS PREPARED FOR BATTLE

When the Devil tried to tempt Jesus, He spoke Scripture to him (Luke 4:1–13). Even though He was the Word of God, He still spoke it out loud to the enemy. We will need to speak the Word of God out loud at times in order for the enemy to flee. No matter how spiritual we are, trials are inevitable. He does promise to be with us and that we can be more than a conqueror through Him; and that also includes conquering our minds.

Do we believe our feelings more than the Word of God? We have to determine how we will react to our feelings before they even happen. We have to choose to believe that God's love, goodness, and promises are greater than any mistakes or problems we face, and we have to be prepared to combat the contradicting thoughts to the Word of God with the Word of God.

What do soldiers do when they get ready for battle? They train, build their muscles, and put on special gear. What should we do as Christian soldiers preparing for the Devil's attacks? Put on the Word of God. Build our faith muscles. Put on our gear: the armor of God. The weak fall in battle. They will be targeted and trampled by the enemy. It is the skilled and strong soldiers who survive and thrive. Build your faith muscles and your Word muscles so you will win the battle in your mind.

TAKE YOUR MIND CAPTIVE

One of the best things you can do as a single woman to be strong and walk with a noble identity in Christ is to learn to control your thought process and refuse to internalize and believe the lies of the enemy.

What does God say about you? He says He has a plan for you.

He says your ways are not His ways. He says that you have been created for a purpose. He says that you were wonderfully and fearfully made. He says that He knows how to give good gifts to His children. And He says that those who wait upon the Lord shall renew their strength and mount up on wings like eagles. That is symbolic, saying that you will soar to greater heights than you imagined when you wait on Him.

So here are a few tips in regard to controlling your mind:

1. Stop having pity parties.

When you begin to get down about some past offense, snap yourself out of it and go do something good for yourself!

2. Make a conscious choice to stop allowing your past to victimize you.

Be present in the present. Focus on what you do have, who you are, and who God is molding you to be.

3. Speak Scripture over your negative thoughts.

Turn your negative emotions into positive ones. This means you need to memorize a few uplifting Scriptures or have them available on your phone or in a journal where you can access them at any time of the day. For a great list of inspirational verses, look at the power Scriptures at the end of the book. Satan can't read our thoughts, so speak these Scriptures out loud. Because Satan can't operate through praise or the Word of God, he will flee when confronted with the Word!

CHAPTER 12: ALIGNING YOUR MIND
REFLECTION QUESTIONS:

1. No matter your past, you are not damaged goods, you are not a failure, and you are not doomed to repeat the same mistakes. When we get down on ourselves, we must align our mind with God's Word and take our thoughts captive, even those negative thoughts that say, "You can't do this." God says you can do all things through Christ who gives you strength (and ability) (Phil. 4:13). Of the Scripture listed in this chapter or the back of the book, pick one verse and memorize it so that when

you're tempted by negative thoughts, you can quickly replace it with God's thoughts instead.

2. Pastor Will Bowen came up with a creative way to help his congregation keep positive thoughts on top by wearing purple bracelets. If you struggle with recurring negative thoughts, think of something you can wear—a piece of jewelry you can switch from hand to hand or a rubber band you can place around your wrist—that is a visual reminder to maintain control over your mind. If you catch yourself thinking a negative thought, pop the rubber band or move the jewelry and recite your chosen Scripture. You've got this!

13

Facing the Lonely Giant

"By his light I walked through darkness."
(JOB 29:3 NIV)

Loneliness may be a state of life, but it doesn't have to be a state of mind.

If you are going to take the journey of becoming the amazing woman God designed you to be and give up on the cycle of dating and settling to wait on God's best for you, then you have to know how to conquer loneliness. In my opinion, that is the number-one battle for a single person to overcome. It is a feeling that will visit you often when you are single.

We all get lonely at times. Even married people can feel lonely in a marriage! I speak from experience in that arena. As social beings, most of us crave rewarding social contact and relationships. However, loneliness is not the same as being alone.

You might be surrounded by loads of people and still be lonely. Loneliness can have a significant impact on your mental health, and it can contribute to mental health problems, such as depression. Having a mental health problem can also make you feel lonely. For example, you may be in a state of life right now where you find social contact difficult or find it hard to maintain friendships, or you may feel isolated because of discrimination. Loneliness has many different causes and affects people differently. Often people feel lonely because of their personal circumstances. But sometimes loneliness is a deeper, more constant feeling that comes from within. So how do we learn to conquer feeling lonely?

HOW TO MANAGE FEELINGS OF LONELINESS

Certain lifestyles and the stresses of daily life can make some people socially isolated and vulnerable to loneliness. There are many situations that might make you feel isolated or lonely.

For example, if you:

- Lose a partner or someone close to you
- Go through a relationship breakup
- Are a single parent or caring for someone else, and you find it hard to maintain a social life
- Move to a new area without family, friends, or community networks
- Are excluded from social activities because of mobility problems or a shortage of money
- Experience discrimination and stigma because of a disability or long-term health condition, or your gender, race, or sexuality
- Have experienced sexual or physical abuse and find it hard to form close relationships with other people

You might feel unable to like yourself or to be liked by others, or you may lack self-confidence. This may come from having been unloved as a child so that, as an adult, you continue to feel unlovable in all relationships. Or sometimes, consciously or unconsciously, people isolate themselves within their relationships because they are afraid of being hurt.

These are all legitimate reasons to feel isolated and lonely. But you can still take steps—or just one step—to reach out to others and to begin to change your circumstances. Loneliness can most of the time be fought and overcome if we change our mindset and focus.

TIPS TO OVERCOME LONELINESS[9,10]

1. Don't isolate.

When you're feeling lonely already, it can be hard to think about trying to engage with other people, but keeping your own company may only make the problem worse. Loneliness often comes from people not feeling comfortable letting other people close to them. If you have a negative self-image, you may be afraid to let others get to know you for fear they might not like what they find. "If you can't let people close to you, however, you are going to feel alone." The problem, social worker Brock Hansen explains, is that when you isolate, there's nobody around to challenge your negative self-image. "You have no reality checks—you only have your own view of yourself."

If you are struggling with a negative self-image, please go buy the book by Beth Moore called *So Long Insecurity*. It will make a huge difference in how you see yourself.

2. Keep busy.

Though it may be the last thing you want to do if you're feeling isolated, join a group—a book club, a sports team, a choir or a gardening group, for example—where you can meet people who share your interests. If you join a group where the activity is meaningful for you, and you enjoy it, chances are it will bring out the best in you. And if you feel good while you're engaged in that activity, it will help you feel more connected to the people around you because you have this one thing in common.

To conquer loneliness, you have to move beyond yourself. Find a purpose. Find an organization such as a soup kitchen or Meals on Wheels and donate your time to it. Go visit people in the hospital or nursing homes. Join a support group for singles. Buy a book and start a Bible study. There is a world of people hurting and wounded that could use your care and attention. When we stop focusing on ourselves and start doing things for others, our lonely feelings start to diminish.

3. Be kind to yourself.

If you're chronically lonely, you may be fearful of letting people get close. First, learn to love yourself! Fixing a negative view of yourself takes a lot of gentle self-care and nurturing. The first relationship you need to work on is your relationship with yourself—and that may mean gently correcting ways of thinking you learned as a child. For example, if you were neglected or criticized, you need to turn that around. You need to start treating yourself differently. The biggest challenge is to treat yourself well when you aren't feeling good about yourself. Being happier with yourself will make it easier to reach out to others.

4. Get educated.

Emily White started writing her book on loneliness because she was curious to know more about her condition. Her research actually helped her to feel less lonely by making it less mysterious, which made it easier to deal with. "The more you learn about loneliness and how common it is, the less alone you feel," she explains. "It's hard to be lonely, but it's harder when you don't understand it or you feel alone in your loneliness."

If you can't seem to shake the feeling of loneliness, try talking to a pastor or church member. Reach out to someone. The worst thing you can do is retreat during your loneliness.

5. Realize that loneliness is a feeling, not a fact.

When you are feeling lonely, it is because something has triggered a memory of that feeling, not because you are in fact isolated and alone. The brain is designed to pay attention to pain and danger, and that includes painful, scary feelings; therefore, loneliness gets our attention.

But then the brain tries to make sense of the feeling. *Why am I feeling this way? Is it because nobody loves me? Because I am a loser. Because they are all mean.* Theories about why you are feeling lonely can become confused with facts. Then it becomes a bigger problem, so just realize that you are having this feeling that will pass and accept it without overreacting.

6. Reach out.

Because loneliness is painful and can confuse you into thinking that you are a loser and an outcast, you might react by with-drawing into yourself, your thoughts, and your lonely feelings, and this is not helpful. At its best, anticipation of loneliness might motivate us to reach out and cultivate friendships, which is the healthiest thing to do if you are sad and alone.

7. Notice your self-deflating thoughts.

Pay attention to your thoughts. Making an intentional effort to stop yourself when negative thoughts come into your mind is the first step to changing your thought patterns. Just as I mentioned in the last chapter, you have to control what you allow your mind to focus on, or it will control you. Chances are you aren't even aware of how many negative or unflattering thoughts you think about yourself or your situation each day. Correcting your mind-set is a great first step to overcoming loneliness.

8. Make a plan to fight the mental and emotional habits of loneliness.

If you realize you are dealing with an emotional habit, you can make a plan to deal with loneliness. Since healthy interaction with friends is good, make some effort to reach out to others and to initiate conversation and face time even when your lone-liness and depression are telling you not to. Yes, it is work, but it is worthwhile, just like exercising is worthwhile even when you are feeling tired.

9. Focus on the needs and feelings of others.

You can walk down the street thinking about yourself, your loneliness, and the hopelessness of it all while staring at the side-walk and sighing. Or you can walk down the street grateful for the diversity of people and silently wishing them good health and good fortune while you are thankful for your own. We choose how to view our situations. In addition to doing this, start notic-ing all the places that could use an extra hand. There are so many needy people, ministries, businesses, and more that could use your help. When we get beyond ourselves and give of ourselves, instead of focusing on ourselves, things will begin to change. I once knew a single lady who decided to volunteer her Saturday free time to Habitat for Humanity. While she was out being a blessing to others, guess who she met? Her future husband, who was also a volunteer.

10. Find others like you.

Nowadays there are more tools than ever before to find out where the knitters, hikers, bakers, painter, or dancers are congregating so that you can get together with those who share your interests. This makes it much easier to identify groups with which you will have something in common, a natural basis for beginning a friendship.

One thing I did to overcome my feelings of loneliness when I had decided to focus on bettering myself and not dating anymore was to join a church and dive into all the activities I could. I made new friends, I grew spiritually, and I felt like I belonged somewhere. I started joining small groups in people's homes, and I began to feel like I had a church family.

> *"Don't make important decisions*
> *from a place of loneliness. When you finally*
> *come to yourself, bad decisions will enhance loneliness."*
> —LOAMMI DIAZ

If you are not involved in church, I strongly urge you to find one. Fight any negative feelings you may be having, such as "churches are for married couples," or "I feel like an outsider because I am divorced and I am afraid people will judge me." Girl, we all have issues. If anyone judges you, that is their problem. Do not let any internal feelings keep you from finding a place to belong. Being part of church will make a huge difference in your life.

Remember that loneliness is a state of emotions. It is not a state of being. No matter how lonely you feel, know that it is still a far better state to be in than to be recovering from a broken heart or the emotional baggage of one more unhealthy relationship.

And remember to keep speaking the Word of God over your emotions. Overcome feelings of loneliness with positive thinking, prayer, and the Word of God.

CHAPTER 13: FACING THE LONELY GIANT
REFLECTION QUESTIONS:

1. Feeling lonely at times is normal, especially after a breakup, a loss, or an unexpected event. Take some time to grieve the loss (depending on the loss this can be days or weeks), but then begin to reach up and out to others, accepting help when it is offered and asking friends and family for their support and time. Below, list two or three ways that you normally respond (or have responded in the past) to episodes of loss and change that could use some improvement.

2. Now make a list of alternative actions or responses you can take that allow you to process the emotions in a more positive and life-giving way.

3. This is also a perfect time to use your list of Scripture or positive affirmations! Below, list your absolute favorite feel-good quote. It can be Scripture; a line from a poem, song, or book; or even a quote from a famous person or a family member. Make sure you choose a quote that makes you smile every time you see it.

14

Dating the Smart, Healthy Way

*"Commit your work to the LORD,
and your plans will be established."*
(Proverbs 16:3 ESV)

Unhealthy people attract unhealthy people. If you want to attract a healthy man of character and quality, you must first become what it is that you seek. You have to be healthy (emotionally and mentally) to attract healthy. To have a healthy relationship, you must set—and maintain and enforce—boundaries.

Maybe you have been single a while, and you have spent a great deal of time working on personal issues and personal growth, and you really want to see if a friendship will lead to more. There is a nice guy at work that you have been admiring from a distance, so you invite him to lunch. Sparks fly, and you decide to go out during the weekend. Suddenly, your hopes are up, and as you get ready for the date there is that hope and wonder in the back of your mind. *Could this turn into more?*

Maybe you are tired of being alone for so long. You want to get out and meet people so you decide to join a dating website. It is hard to be single for a long time when your desire is to get married. We simply get tired of watching everyone else fall in love and get married while we still have to be alone. I get it. Being single can often feel like a long boring road to walk on, and at times it is hard. There is nothing wrong with meeting new people, but you have to have a certain mindset and a "shield" around you when you do.

Although there are some great Christian dating websites, because of my personal experience, my philosophy is this: Wait on God to orchestrate the meeting of your future mate and stay off dating websites. While you are waiting, work on becoming the best woman you can be by seeking to develop your character and strength and relationship with Christ. Get busy serving others and being His hands and feet. Establish a vision and purpose as a single woman, and find contentment in your heavenly Husband. When He sees that a work in you has been competed, as well as in your future mate, He will bring the two of you together. Even if that means you have to wait until you are older. Wouldn't you rather wait for His best and experience the abundant life He has planned for you?

I do not expect everyone to agree with my philosophy. I know there are many people who have met someone wonderful through dating websites and are extremely happy. In fact, I know two ladies who met wonderful men from dating websites, and they are happily married to devoted Christians, but these men are often rare. I also know that these women had very high standards and would not settle for anything less than a godly man. They are grounded in the Lord and emotionally healthy women. So they saw their dating website experiences as "interviews." If a man did not have the character they were looking for, they walked away. They didn't keep dating someone just to fill a void and to run from being alone, and they did not let sexual intimacy fall into the dating equation. It took a few years of dating interviews until they finally met someone they were compatible with who had the spiritual maturity they were seeking.

If you are a firm believer in dating websites, then follow your heart, but do yourself a favor—go into each situation with extreme caution. There are a lot of men on dating websites who are fresh out of a relationship and are just looking for a void filler, someone to take their mind off their hurt. There are also a lot of men who are looking to have their physical needs met more than they are looking for something meaningful.

I encourage you to not make it your life mission to *find a man*. Make it a mission to *find yourself in Christ* and to possess an amazing inner beauty first. Become a healthy and whole woman in Christ.

Being internally healthy means many things. Healthy means that you are free from any bondage of your past, with no unresolved anger toward someone who hurt you. You are also free from issues that will affect a new relationship, and are able to see your worth and value in Jesus. Healthy is also loving yourself more than loving a relationship where someone treats you badly and does not respect you. A healthy Christian knows that true happiness comes from within and from faith in Jesus, not from another person.

When you take time to work on inner growth and become content being single, you will grow into a more healthy person who will radiate beauty. You will not want to settle for anything less than God's best for you because you know you are a woman who is worthy of being highly valued.

I recently heard a heart-breaking story from a friend. The thirty-eight-year-old woman got to the point where she began to panic because she was still single and her biological clock was running out. She met someone from a dating website and started dating him. He romanced her, and she fell for him. Over several months' time, his true nature came out, and now she is caught in an abusive relationship where she is hit and threatened often. Being impatient and lacking trust in God's best timing for her put her in a situation that she will have many scars from, and she will have to go through healing when—and if—she finally breaks free. This is what I mean by the enemy using people in our lives to destroy us and get us off the path God wants us to be on. One of the number-one ways the enemy will try and derail a single woman's life is through unhealthy and destructive relationships. So be careful and be aware!

RESPECT YOURSELF

When you do decide to go out and socialize with single men, regardless of where you meet someone, be smart about it and go in with the utmost respect for yourself and with boundaries around you. Don't act like a lost puppy desperate to find someone who will claim you and give you attention. No man will ever have respect and desire for a woman he feels is desperate. Go into every dating situation with a certain perspective. Don't look to a man wondering if he will like you and if you are what he is looking for. Go into each dating situation with this question in mind: "Is this man God's best for me, and does he have what it takes to match me and my character and standards?" Be picky, ladies! Don't mistake that for being arrogant and unrealistic. If you are not picky and don't have standards, it will lead to settling, which will then lead to heartache. If in the first few dates, you find out that you do not have the same views and desires and beliefs, don't stay hoping they will change to match yours.

Don't ever go into a relationship because you think the guy has potential and what you don't like you will change or fix. I have tried that, and it doesn't work. When I married my children's father, my plan was to fix him, but it never worked. His priorities were still his priorities and his ways were still his ways. Someone does not change unless they want to and see the need to. When God has the right one for you, one that He has purposed you to be with, you will not have to fix him or wait until he is on the "same page" as you are.

Intimacy too soon builds a premature bond that will overshadow the type of bonds that should be built in the earlier stages by friendship and companionship. Don't sleep with someone until you are ready to commit for life. As hard as this may be, do not sacrifice the immediate and risk ruining the potential for an awesome future. Do not give the enemy a door to open in which he can mask your judgment. Once you sleep with someone, you enter into an emotional realm that God never intended for you to be in until marriage. It will create a soul tie that could cloud your judgment, your decisions, and your self-respect. Don't risk it for the sake of pleasure. Build intimacy in a friendship first. And never worry if a man will take off if you don't sleep with him. If he pressures you, he isn't the mature godly man you need to be with. If he takes off, let him. Slam the door behind him and tell yourself that you are too precious and have too much self-respect to let a man pressure you or use you.

The man God has for you will respect your choices. He will gladly be on the same page with you and have the same dating goals as you. If he doesn't, he is not the mature, solid man you need. Again, do not jeopardize the immediate and risk damaging the future. Yes, one of man's basic needs is sex, but you do not want him to desire you because you are a need-filler. You want him to desire you because you have boundaries and because you want to build something with someone that is based on mind and soul substance, not sexual substance.

Make him wait! If you start dating someone that you are supposed to be with, not only will he respect you, but waiting will allow both of you to build something amazing. It is easy to have that "I want to try before I buy" mentality. But if God has intended you to be with someone, do you think He will leave the chemistry detail out? Do you think the personalities, spirituality, and compatibility would line up and be great, but the intimacy department would be lacking? No. When God forms something together, it will be amazing. There are some couples I know who have amazing marriages that have lasted a long time, and they decided to abstain from sex when they were dating. They built a solid relationship on soul intimacy instead of physical intimacy, and it made their marriage stronger.

Ladies, sex does not hold a marriage together. What makes a marriage is how you treat each other, how you weather the storms of life together, how you respect one another, how you handle one another's emotions and flaws, and how well you communicate through it all, and much more. These aspects of a relationship cannot be properly built in a dating relationship that has a foundation built on physical intimacy.

Physical intimacy too soon can certainly cloud the ability for growth in the areas of compatibility, communication, mutual respect, patience, friendship, and Christ (spiritual compatibility). If you are dating someone you are supposed to be with, you will have a lifetime to create sexual intimacy. Spend your dating season creating intimacy in friendship and in spirituality. When you do this, you will be building something that can last a lifetime.

I say it again, do not succumb to the immediate pleasures and jeopardize the future. And wouldn't it be very special to offer the gifts of yourselves to each other on your wedding night? No doubt this would take a lot of self-discipline, but imagine how amazingly special it would be!

Looking back on my dating website experiences, I wish I could say I went into each one with caution and had definite boundaries set—but I didn't. I think I had an invisible sign on the back of my shirt that said, "Desperate and Dateless. Come Save Me." And I sadly and shamefully admit that there were a few men who picked up on it and played me. Of course I ended up with regret and picked myself up and moved on. But I wasn't whole then. I was empty, looking for love and security in a man. Looking back now on that time in my life, I realize not only did I not demand respect from a man by my actions, I didn't have the respect I needed for myself to set boundaries. So when the shallow romance ended, I was left feeling cheap, used, and angry at both the man and myself.

We are human, and yes, we have needs, but don't put your needs before having wisdom and having respect for yourself. Before getting involved with anyone, set boundaries. Draw imaginary lines in your dating life. You hear people say, "Guard your heart." Well, it is sticking to the boundaries that will allow you to guard your heart. Standards plus boundaries will create a demand for respect, a healthier you, and a healthier relationship.

WHAT DOES IT MEAN TO HAVE BOUNDARIES?

Boundaries are physical, emotional, sexual, and mental limits we set in relationships to protect us from being controlled, manipulated, abused, or taken advantage of. As John Stibbs explains, "They make it possible for us to separate our own thoughts and feelings from those of others and to take responsibility for what we think, feel and do."[11] They make it possible for us to accept no from others and to say no to ourselves. They enable us to make choices about how we feel, think, or behave. They help draw a line between "me" and "you."

Personal boundaries should be designed to help us. They are standards, like the ones I list below, that we establish for ourselves so we know what we will and will not put up with. Boundaries are for our personal security both physically and mentally.

Before you start dating, you have to establish your own personal boundaries. These are things you are willing to accept and not accept. These are just a few examples of boundaries, though there can be many; and there again, you can set as many personal boundaries as you choose.

Here are examples of boundaries that I established for myself. They are in no particular order.

- I will not spend my time dating men who I have to turn into "The Man I Think He Could/Should Be."
- I will not wait around for a man to decide if he wants to be with me—I'm not putting my life on hold for anyone.
- I will not continue engaging in any relationship where they don't treat me with love, care, trust, and respect.
- I will not date someone who controls the relationship on their terms—I must be in mutually fulfilling, balanced, healthy relationships.
- I will not allow someone to use me for sex, devalue me sexually, or treat me in a lesser-than manner.
- I will not date anyone who has poor character—someone who is unkind/cruel, lacking in empathy, takes advantage of me, or abuses me.
- I will not date someone who is not a believer in Jesus Christ.

Since I do not want to be unequally yoked, there is no need in dating someone who does not share my beliefs.

- I will not date anyone who can't respect my free time and give me the freedom to spend time to maintain relationships outside of ours.
- I will not date a man who is not supportive of my dreams, personal goals, and career goals.

WHAT ARE "HEALTHY BOUNDARIES"?[12]

A person with healthy boundaries is able to identify how she feels about something, what she thinks about something, and how she reacts or behaves in a situation. She is able to distinguish between her own emotions, opinions, and behaviors and those of others. And she takes responsibility for them. She does not blame others for how she thinks, feels, or behaves. She is able to stand up for herself calmly and intelligently without intimidation or manipulation. And she has enough love for herself to walk away from an unhealthy situation.

A person with healthy boundaries does not allow other people to control how she thinks, feels, or behaves, nor does she try to control them. She does not play the victim, and she does not tolerate abuse.

A person with healthy boundaries is able to say no when her boundaries are intruded upon. She is able to recognize her own needs, take responsibility for them, and ask for what she needs honestly and openly without mind games. She is able to accept no from others without having her self-esteem shattered.

A person with healthy boundaries has a strong enough sense of self that she doesn't absorb other people's negative emotions or personalize their bad behavior.

WHY ARE HEALTHY BOUNDARIES IMPORTANT IN RELATIONSHIPS?

Successful relationships are composed of two people, each with a clear definition of him or herself. When they share their lives with each other, neither person "loses themselves" in the relationship by becoming so wrapped up in it that the relationship becomes their entire world. A person with healthy boundaries is not a parasite feeding off the other to get their needs met. Some believe that "love" consists of becoming totally absorbed by or engulfed in the other person. This is not "love." True love requires that each person be a healthy individual within themselves before they can form a healthy relationship together.

IF YOU ARE NOT HAPPY ALONE, YOU WILL NOT BE HAPPY IN A RELATIONSHIP

Each person in a relationship needs a clear sense of who they are in order to clearly define and communicate their needs to their partner without manipulation or mind games. You can't do this if you are carrying someone else's emotions, blaming others for your behavior, or practicing someone else's beliefs.

The goal of a solid and healthy relationship is to feel calm, centered, and focused. When we lack these elements in our relationships, it is mainly due to an inability to establish and maintain healthy boundaries. So what could a relationship look like that does not have boundaries, versus one that does?[13]

When you give up your boundaries in a relationship, you:
- Are unclear about your preferences
- Do not notice unhappiness since enduring is your concern
- Alter your behavior, plans, or opinions to fit the current moods or circumstances of another (live reactively)
- Do more and more for less and less
- Live hopefully while wishing and waiting for the person to change
- Are satisfied if you are coping and surviving
- Have few hobbies because you have no attention span for self-directed activity
- Make exceptions for a person for things you would not tolerate in anyone else
- Are manipulated by flattery so you lose objectivity
- Try to create intimacy with a narcissist
- Are so strongly affected by another that obsession results

- Will forsake every personal limit when your partner wants sex
- Act out of compliance and compromise
- Do favors that you inwardly resist (cannot say no)
- Allow your partner to abuse your children or friends
- Mostly feel afraid and confused
- Are enmeshed in drama too often
- Are living a life that is not yours and that seems unalterable
- Commit yourself for as long as the other needs you to be committed (no bottom line)

When your boundaries are intact in a relationship, you:
- Have clear preferences and act upon them
- Recognize when you are happy/unhappy
- Acknowledge moods and circumstances around you while remaining centered
- Trust your own intuition while being open to others' opinions
- Live optimistically while constantly working on change
- Are more satisfied if you are thriving, not digressing
- Are encouraged by sincere, ongoing change for the better
- Have excited interest in self-enhancing hobbies and projects
- Have a personal standard that applies to everyone and asks for accountability
- Relate only to partners with whom mutual love is possible
- Know intimacy is enjoyable but never at the cost of your integrity and personal beliefs
- Let yourself feel anger, and embark upon a program of change
- Act out of agreement and compromise
- Only do favors you choose to do (you can say no)
- Mostly feel secure and clear
- Are always aware of choices
- Decide how, to what extent, and how long you will be committed
- Protect your private matters without having to lie or be surreptitious

DID YOU KNOW MEN TEST OUR BOUNDARIES?

By no means am I downing men in this chapter. Not all men are like this, but a majority are. Men will test your boundaries in dating for one very simple reason: they want to know if you're a woman who respects herself and is all about serious and committed relationships, or if you're a woman to have fun with for the time being.

Unfortunately, there are immature and emotionally unavailable men who will test your boundaries to see whether or not they can get away with enjoying some of the benefits that come with being in a relationship with you, without having to commit. These men will never be interested in having a relationship with you no matter how good your credentials are; they're simply not ready for that right now. They may tell you they are because they want you to fall for them, but they don't have intentions of making long-term commitments to anyone.

Respectable, mature men who want to have a committed and fulfilling relationship will want a woman who's consistent and firm with her boundaries. Most men find it an attractive quality when a woman is sure of her boundaries. He will respect that. It communicates to him how you expect to be treated, what he can and can't get away with, and whether or not it's a challenge he feels up to or can even meet.

So when you do finally meet someone you feel is a good man, the boundaries you set and uphold in dating will play a huge role in helping a man see you as relationship material and not just a woman he wants to be intimate with.

WHAT MEN REALLY WANT

There are three basic needs that apply to all men: food, respect, and sex. I am not saying that this is *all they need*, but these are three universal needs of all men simply because of how they are wired. Please do not go into a dating situation thinking you will get a man to fall for you and want to be with you if you are great at meeting these three needs. Men crave these things, but most men out there want to settle down with someone they know respects and values themselves.

A lot of men like to "play," but when it comes to settling down, they want quality and character, not a woman that numerous men have also "enjoyed." This is one reason why I feel it is so important that while you are single you take some time to develop your character, find your own identity in being alone, and define your boundaries before you start dating for the first time or again. Learn how to let Christ fill your inner needs, because no man can fulfill your soul like Christ can. Being a strong, independent woman is very attractive to men. After all, sticking to boundaries is also a reflection of your self-worth, self-respect, and your self-esteem.

Immature, selfish, and emotionally unavailable men want women they can manipulate and control to their advantage. So if your boundaries in dating are flaky and you end up in a relationship with him [the kind of man I described above], you've likely attracted this type of man through your boundaries, and it will ultimately end up in heartache and regret. Mature and evolved men love to be with women who are very clear and firm about how they wish to be treated.[14]

Have you ever had a single friend who no longer had time for you when she got into a relationship? She took a Boyfriend Hiatus. This is because she didn't have the proper boundaries set. Never, ever change your life completely to accommodate your guy. If you find yourself changing your life to revolve around him, things are going to end badly in the long run. To begin, you aren't "teaching" your man to respect your individual life or make plans in advance. Second, it's not fair to your friends. And finally, the ultimate result of a long-term Boyfriend Hiatus is that if the relationship doesn't work out, you may find yourself deserted on "Friendless Island" as a result of ignoring your relationships for far too long, and that is simply disastrous.

Make sure you don't neglect the life you have! Not only will it ensure men respect you and meet your needs, but it will ensure you always feel complete from the inside out. The famous "You complete me" line in the movie *Jerry Maguire* needs to stay on the big screen where it belongs. Remember: men cannot complete us. Only our Creator can.

Boundaries and self-respect make you more beautiful. By holding firm to your boundaries, not only will men have more respect for you, you will have more respect for yourself. While you are waiting for God to bring you an awesome man, be cautious with every situation you go into. Remember that the enemy knows how highly valued you are to Christ, and you are a threat to him. He will try to derail your life and your destiny by bringing the wrong people across your path. Never let the enemy derail your life because you are desperate and tired of being single.

Highly favored, valued, strong, and chosen Woman of God—do not let your boundaries fall away. Respect, love, and value yourself so that others will do the same.

CHAPTER 14: DATING THE SMART, HEALTHY WAY
REFLECTION QUESTIONS:

1. If you want to attract a healthy man of character and quality, you must first become what is it you seek. You have to be healthy (emotionally and mentally) to attract healthy. First, make a list below of seven to ten healthy qualities you seek in someone else. These can include the items you posted for your non-negotiables, but they can also include personality traits, personal interests, and hobbies.

2. Next, for each item listed, ask yourself, "Do I have a similar or matching quality or interest?" The goal here is not to attract someone exactly like you but to broaden your horizons, especially if you've had the same routine, interests, and hobbies for years.

3. Remember the chapter about red flags? A man who is pushing you to become intimate on the first date (or anytime before you are ready for intimacy, whether physical or emotional) is a red flag! While you can't prevent someone else's poor behavior, you can prepare for it in the event it does happen by creating a checklist for your first few outings together.

a. Wear whatever makes you feel comfortable and beautiful.

b. Establish in your mind what your boundaries are regarding physical closeness, conversation, even the time limit!

c. Pay attention to the way your date treats others including the wait staff (should you go out to eat), other drivers (if he picks you up), and strangers you encounter during the course of the date. However he treats those people is how he will treat you, too.

d. If your date shows any red flags during the course of your time together, do not ignore them!

4. Just say "No." How many times have we accepted a second date with someone even though they said a few things that made us uncomfortable, or we really didn't have a good time on the first date, or we didn't feel any chemistry (physical, emotional, conversational, or otherwise) . . . because they asked?

a. Practice your "No's"! Below, write out five different responses you can give to someone who asks for a date but who does not meet your criteria. (Examples can begin with: "Thank you for asking but…" or "I appreciate the offer, however….")

15

Untangling the Soul Ties

"Guard your heart above all else,
for it determines the course of your life."
(Proverbs 4:23 NLT)

Short-term solutions can create long-term misery. Your choice can affect the rest of the days after. You can no longer afford to be unwise about your choices.

My sweet friend Abigail is twenty-nine and gorgeous. She got married at twenty-four and after two years of marriage, her husband cheated on her with her best friend. They divorced and she moved to Nashville where she never has to see either of them. She is on a mission right now to redefine herself and heal from what she calls being "messed up." She is too afraid to get involved with a man, so she will not allow herself to get too close emotionally. Staying away from commitment while she is working on herself is a good thing. Where she is "playing with fire" is when she acts out through what is most likely a soul tie she is not able to recognize.

Even though she is afraid of getting involved with someone out of fear of being hurt, she is driven by the need for attention and affection from a man. She is gorgeous so she has no problem finding attention when she "needs her fix," as she says. At her work, a married man started showing her attention. Even though she is afraid to get involved with anyone, she says the attention gives her a fix. So she feels a married man is safe for her because he doesn't plan to leave his wife. They just simply have fun together and she is getting the attention and pleasure she wants without being emotionally involved.

I warned her about this dangerous situation, how wrong it is, and the damage it could lead to for both of them. What she doesn't want to realize is that by sleeping with this man, she is becoming connected through soul ties. Soul ties can be dangerous and lead to destruction. I speak from experience on this. I had to break some ungodly soul ties that I realized were there from my past relationships. These soul ties were keeping me from being spiritually and emotionally healthy.

WHAT IS A SOUL TIE?

The topic of soul ties is not something that a lot of churches speak about, but they are very real. In fact, some people argue against such things as a soul tie because they think there is no biblical evidence of one existing between two people. The Bible does not come out and call it a soul tie, but God says that David and Jonathan's souls were knit together (1 Samuel 18:1). They had a friendship so deep that their souls connected. Soul ties can be created in a friendship, between a husband and wife, and between parents and children. These are loving bonds, and there is nothing wrong with these soul ties.

What I am talking about are the soul ties that are created in an unhealthy relationship that God did not intend for you to be in. These would include ties that were created through intimacy when you dated or had a fling with a man you settled for, or should have never been with because it wasn't a God-honoring situation.

When sexual intimacy occurs, a soul tie is formed because that is how God designed the human being. There are people out there who have sex very freely; one-night stands are not given a second thought. These types of people are at a great risk of many things beyond multiple soul ties; they are at risk of becoming calloused to what God designed true intimacy for, not to mention the risk of unplanned pregnancy and STDs! Ladies, *run* if you meet a guy who views sex as just something casual and fun. If that's the case, then you know he is willing to play with *anyone*. Do not subject your emotional or physical health to this kind of careless behavior.

WHEN TWO BECOME ONE

God designed for man and woman to become one. This means that sex joins man and woman in a deeper way than what just a friendship does. There is an act that takes place when two human bodies connect through the act of sex. When a man enters a woman's body, their souls become connected in the spiritual realm whether they want them to or not. Soul ties between married couples draw them together like magnets, while soul ties between unmarried couples can draw an abused woman to a man she would otherwise run from. She runs to him even though he mistreats and lies to her over and over. This woman thinks she can change this man. And it is the soul tie that keeps this woman going back over and over to the man who mistreats her and does not respect her.

This may seem really far-fetched for some people who have not read about or been taught about the spiritual forces combating against each other, but demonic spirits are real. The Bible speaks in many places about Jesus speaking to demons in people or casting them out of people. If you are a believer in Jesus, a demonic spirit cannot possess you, but it can attack you and sometimes cloud your judgment. In the demonic world, unholy soul ties can serve as bridges between two people to pass demonic garbage through. When a soul tie occurs, the spirits that could be attacking them individually will have the ability to pass between the bond created.

Looking back at the time I was twenty-three and met the man who conned me, I know without a doubt that a demonic soul tie was drawing me to him. I was so masked by a spirit of deception that my judgment was squandered. I look back now and wonder how I could have been so gullible. I simply was not myself around him, but I didn't realize that until later on.

Have you ever had a friend who started dating someone and she really changed (and not always for the best)? I am talking about the kind of situation where you ask yourself, *What happened to her? She wasn't like that before.* She likely changed due to soul ties. If she was in an unhealthy relationship that changed her, it is because a soul tie opened a bridge for demonic spirits to pass and they are now attacking her.

We live in a world full of angels and demons that we simply can't see. Demonic spirits try to influence us often. Their goal is to destroy people mentally and emotionally, and Satan's number-one goal is to build his kingdom. Therefore, he attacks believers so he can oppress them, bind them, and get their eyes off their God and His purpose for them. They come in doors we open such as resentment, anger, unforgiveness, lust, and criticism. (The Bible talks of many different spirits that can attack us. Research it if you are more interested in specifics.)

Another example of a soul tie in the Bible is in 1 Corinthians 6:16: "Do you not know that he who unites himself with a prostitute is one with her in body? For it is said, 'The two will become one flesh'" (NIV). Obviously the two didn't get married, but something spiritual happened when they were joined physically in the act of sex. They were "joined"; their souls were "tied." Often people who commit fornication or adultery still think about that person years later. That is because a soul tie has been created. And they can last for years.

I battled for a few months over an ungodly soul tie created from one of my short-term relationships after my divorce. Satan still ties to remind me of it at times even as a married woman, but I have learned how to come against it through prayer and with the Word.

So soul ties are very real. The good news is we have authority over these spirits. The Holy Spirit in us has dominion and power over anything the enemy tries to inflict on us. The secret is being able to rise up and walk in the authority we have as daughters of Christ.

Here is what the Word says regarding fighting these demonic spirits:

> Finally, be strong in the Lord and in his mighty power. Put on the full armor of God, so that you can take your stand against the devil's schemes. For our struggle is not against flesh and blood, but against the rulers, against the authorities, *against the powers of this dark world and against the spiritual forces of evil in the heavenly realms.* Therefore put on the full armor of God, so that when the day of evil comes, you may be able to stand your ground, and after you have done everything, to stand. Stand firm then, with the belt of truth buckled around your waist, with the breastplate of righteousness in place, and with your feet fitted with the readiness that comes from the gospel of peace. *In addition to all this, take up the shield of faith, with which you can extinguish all the flaming arrows of the evil one.* Take the helmet of salvation and the sword of the Spirit, which is the word of God. And pray in the Spirit on all occasions with all kinds of prayers and requests. With this in mind, be alert and always keep on praying for all the Lord's people. (EPHESIANS 6:10–18 NIV, MY EMPHASIS ADDED)

We have to be alert and aware so that we can not only stand against our enemy, but not become trapped and blinded. This is why I stressed in the last chapter to be smart and cautious in every dating relationship you enter. Take a good amount of time to get to know who they are and what they struggle with before you ever become romantically involved with them. Get to know their character and their depth of spirituality. Do not put yourself in a situation that could enable the enemy to create a bridge for a damaging soul tie to pass.

HEALING FROM SOUL TIES

In Luke 13:10–13, we read about a woman who sat in a preaching service, and the Word says she had had a spirit of infirmity for eighteen years: "On a Sabbath Jesus was teaching in one of the synagogues, and a woman was there who had been crippled by a spirit for eighteen years. She was bent over and could not straighten up at all. When Jesus saw her, he called her forward and said to her, 'Woman, you are set free from your infirmity.' Then he put his hands on her, and immediately she straightened up and praised God" (NIV). Verse 16 says, "Then should not this woman, a daughter of Abraham [a man of faith], whom Satan has kept bound for eighteen long years, be set free on the Sabbath day from what bound her?" Demonic spirits cannot possess a Christian, but they can certainly bind us and keep us from experiencing the freedom and abundant life God wants for us. I am talking about spirits such as depression, low self-esteem, anger, bitterness, mental weakness, sexual addiction, and more.

Having an ungodly soul tie does not mean you are a bad person. It just means that there is something buried in you that is not meant to be there, and it is keeping you from being the woman God has designed you to be and longs for you to be.

Maybe you have scars and wounds lodged in your soul that may have been there for years. You can be bound by something you don't even realize you are bound by. You need to get before God and ask Him to heal you of wounds and reveal soul ties you may not recognize.

So you may ask, "Why doesn't God just heal me of anything that binds me?" He will and He does, but you have to go forth. Just as Jesus called His daughter forth in the synagogue in Luke 13 and set her free, He is calling us forth. We just have to go forth!

You may also be asking, "How do I know I have an ungodly soul tie?" If there is anything that has control over your life or torments your life in any way that contradicts the Word of God, it can be a soul tie. It can even be a memory that haunts you.

God will take out whatever you ask Him to, but in order for you to find healing and release from any type of bondage or soul tie the enemy has placed on you, you have to first identify it and renounce it. Confront your soul matters and be real with yourself, no matter how painful it is. You cannot conquer what you don't take time to identify! And you can't conquer what you don't confront.

Write down the names of individuals that you had relationships with that led to ungodly behavior. If you have been raped or cannot recall the names of each person, do the best you can. Then take this list into a prayer closet if you have to. Shout and stomp on it if you must. You can go into warfare in private and act in whatever way you need to find deliverance. Come against your enemy and fight him with the authority God already says you have. Speak the Word against your enemy and cripple him. Then take this list before God. Denounce everything and everyone on your list. Ask God to break you from the bondage, the memories, the self-condemnation, and the emotional dependence that may exist. For every action you take in Jesus' name, there will be a reaction from God! This is a promise from Him.

RENOUNCE EACH SOUL TIE

You'll want to break the soul tie in Jesus' name using your authority in Him. Do this verbally so that it has an impact! Here's an example:

> "In Jesus' name, I now renounce any ungodly soul ties formed between myself and (the person's name) as a result of (the action). I now break and sever any ungodly soul ties formed between myself and (the person's name) as a result of (sexual sin, emotional dependence, abuse, codependency, etc.) in Jesus' name."

Now what do you do with the list? You discard it, burn it, or tear it up, and remove it from your presence completely. Let the past be the past.

And what about any items you may still have from any of these men? Here's some great advice to consider:

If gifts were given to you by the other person in connection with the sin or unholy relationship, such as rings, flowers, cards, or even lingerie, etc. Get rid of them! Such things symbolize the ungodly relationship, and can hold a soul tie in place.

Any rash vows or commitments made that played a part in forming the soul tie should be renounced and repented of, and broken in Jesus' name. Even things like "I will love you forever," or "I could never love another man!" need to be renounced. They are spoken commitments that need to be undone verbally.[15]

You must also forgive that person if you have anything against them. This may be hard, but ask God to give you the grace you need for the other person.

You may have to go through several times of warfare and renouncing soul ties. The enemy does not want you to be free from the bondage, and he will try to inflict you with doubts and guilt again. But that is when you put on your armor again and go into spiritual warfare. You may have to do this daily for a while. That is okay! Do whatever you have to do to find a healthy and whole you.

AVOID SOUL TIES IN THE FUTURE

The best way to avoid soul ties is to refrain from sex until a commitment has been made—a lasting commitment. If you are meant to be with someone, sacrificing a year of your life or more to build a solid foundation that will last is nothing.

Become a foundation builder, not a try-before-you-buy shopper. When you have this mindset, you will avoid soul ties, save yourself a lot of heartache and regret, and be able to think through dating situations with your head and not with emotions. Because once you have sex, ties are created that you may not realize are there.

If you want to read more on this topic, I highly recommend *Seductions Exposed: The Spiritual Dynamics of Relationships* by Dr. Gary L. Greenwald. This book takes you behind the scenes of soul ties, transferring of spirits, and how the enemy can use various things to gain a bridge into our souls.

CHAPTER 15: UNTANGLING THE SOUL TIES
REFLECTION QUESTIONS:

1. Soul ties are real and they can be powerful bonds to the past. Thankfully, they can be broken. In this chapter, I encouraged you to make a list of your soul ties, remembering that these can be created through sexual acts and deep friendships. After making the list, I encouraged you to renounce each tie and discard the list. If you did not participate in that exercise, please consider doing so now.

2. Good riddance! Next we must get rid of any items we were given during the course of that relationship, including gifts, jewelry, cards…even any articles of their clothing we may still have. Here's where you may feel resistance, especially if you're being asked to get rid of jewelry or other particularly meaningful (or valuable) items. There's no reason to throw items away if you don't have to—instead donate them or sell them!

   a. If you have jewelry, take it to your local pawn shop (or two) and let it go. Then use the money to do something nice for yourself!

   b. If you have items such as clothing or homegoods, donate them to Goodwill where someone else can benefit from their use.

   c. If you have any pictures, cards, or other paper goods, have a shredding party! You can even invite some friends over to do this together if you feel company would help lighten the mood.

Section Four:
Celebrating Your Purpose

*"And we know that in all things God works
for the good of those who love him, who have
been called according to his purpose."*
(ROMANS 8:28 NIV)

16
Single Moms Empowered!

"I can do all this through him who gives me strength."
(PHILIPPIANS 4:13 NIV)

I couldn't write this book without offering a word of hope and encouragement to the single moms. The years I was a single mom to two young children were some of the hardest I ever faced. But in those years, I grew closer to God than ever before because I ran to Him more than ever before! I learned how to rely on Him as my heavenly Husband, the One who made me whole. I didn't fully learn this until I walked away from the dating scene and began to seek God wholeheartedly. But when I sought wholeness and learned to really trust Him and rely on Him, I found contentment like I had never known as a single woman and single mom.

I understand the financial struggles, the feeling of being overwhelmed because you are doing everything alone, the feelings of loneliness that try to visit you often, and the feeling like you really have no place to belong in a society of so many couples. I had so many mixed emotions as I faced the burdens of being a single mom. Do not try to go through these hardships alone.

On top of hardships that come with being a single mom, there were times I was an emotional mess because of the hurt and disappointment from failed relationships. I tried my best not to let my kids see it, but they sensed something was not right with me. In the three years after my divorce, when I was on the man hunt, I am thankful I stuck to the decision to never introduce my children to someone unless it developed into something serious. I only dated on the weekends they were gone to their father's house. I wanted to shelter my kids from seeing their mom dating different men, but they knew I was seeing people because I was on the phone talking or texting often, and at times, my attention was not fully on them.

I regret that now. I regret the fact that I lost valuable time with my children by being distracted by men who I knew deep down were not God's best for me.

IT'S A SEASON, NOT A SENTENCE

We all have a story of how we ended up here. For some, it was by choice. For others, it was by an upheaval followed by an unraveling. Whatever walk of life you come from—divorced, abandoned, widowed, single, or never married—stop right now as you read this and tell yourself that you are amazing. And don't just say it; believe it!

We have moments and sometimes days where we want to hide in the bathtub in an effort to soak away the feelings of frustration and being overwhelmed, but regardless of our emotions, at the end of every day when the lights are out and the house is still, *we are still awesome.* You may not feel like it as you are bombarded with all the "should haves," but in spite of what we feel we are lacking, *we are still awesome.*

We are awesome for walking in bravery in this world and taking each day and challenge with our subconscious drive telling us, "I've got to do this on my own." We are awesome for persevering because we know we have no choice, and we are awesome for carrying the weight on our shoulders and still being able to catch our children when they fall because we know we have to.

It is not easy being a single mom in our society. We are often labeled and made to feel we don't fit in. Our children are labeled as being "from a broken home" like we operate in some realm of dysfunction or represent that which is not normal. But I am here to tell you that the same Spirit of God who dwells in the homes of married couples will dwell in your home if you invite Him in.

Regardless of what we feel the world sees, God sees us with the same eyes of love, mercy, compassion, and grace as He sees others. The same blood of Jesus that covers the family and places a hedge of protection around them will cover you and your children.

Single moms, I want to encourage you to have a certain mindset about your single-mom life. This is a season of your life. It may feel like a long season, but it is a valuable season because *you are everything to your children.* I know how easy it is to feel like you are in overdrive and survival mode, but do everything you can to keep yourself mentally and physically healthy. They need a healthy mom who is strong and whom they feel is totally invested in them. You will never get back the critical foundational years of their life, meaning birth through age eighteen. God has entrusted you with the life or lives of His precious masterpieces, and God will give you the wisdom and strength you need as you parent them alone.

As loving moms, we want our children to grow up and have an awesome future. Their childhood is their foundation. What they learn and see in their childhood and how they are raised will determine the type of adults they grow up to be, and you can still build a loving foundation and provide a good example to them as a single parent.

The mindset I encourage you to have is this: Trust that in time, God will meet your needs in the man department, but until He does, make meeting your kids' needs your number-one priority. Determine you will be the best single mom that you can be, and pour into their lives as you rely on Jesus to pour into yours.

It is hard to wait when you long for companionship, but wait for God to bring you what you and your kids need, and don't try to find it yourself. I promise you that when you wait on God, it will not only be amazing for you but great for your kids as well. It takes a special man to be a loving and influential stepfather. Don't try to find him yourself. Let God do it. If you do decide to date, have boundaries and use extreme caution because your decisions will affect more than just your own life and emotions.

You also have to reach a point mentally where you are okay with being a single mom. It may not be meant for you to have a husband and stepfather for your kids while they are young. God may not bring someone into your life until your kids are older. You have to get to a point where you can accept that. When you can accept it, it is easier to find contentment.

Isn't it better to *wait* for something wonderful than to settle for something that may bring hurtful consequences and scars for you and for your children's lives? I have heard stories of women (and even men) who were devastated by the actions of their stepfather. How sad for those mothers to know that their decisions to settle for less than a godly man left scars in their children's lives that they will carry into adulthood. How sad for those children that they have to carry the memories and scars with them into their adulthood and have to seek healing because their mom did not make a good choice.

One of my friends is dealing with this now—in her adult years—because her mother got remarried to a man after she was grown up and married herself. The new husband forces my friend's mother to steal pills from the pharmacy where she works so he can use and sell them. You would think that this woman would leave him, but she is in bondage with soul ties, and she cannot break free. And it causes great stress and anxiety in my friend, knowing that her mother is in a bad relationship and performing illegal activities at the insistence of her ungodly husband!

Unfortunately, this scenario plays out over and over in the lives of so many women and mothers under the spell of a dysfunctional relationship. So during this season of being a single mom, remember that your choices, your mindset, and your love will be displayed to your children and will influence them.

BEAT THE STRUGGLES . . . AT LEAST IN YOUR MIND

As a single mom, something that drove me to do my best even when I was worn out and longed for some "me time" was the thought that one day I will stand before my Father and He will ask me what I did with the valuable lives He entrusted to me. I do not want to stand before Him and be ashamed because I messed their lives up more than they already were from being from a broken home. I never want my kids to end up in a counselor's office as an adult because they have to work through something I did to them or inflicted upon them as a child, apart from leaving their father. This mindset often kept me going. I have made mistakes and am not perfect, but I can at least say I am working on doing my best.

I feel the hardest thing about being a single mom is the burden that you feel you carry alone. It is a financial burden, a responsibility burden, and an emotional burden that can easily create weariness. When I was a single mom and full-time school teacher, I got up every school morning at 5 a.m. to make myself a cup of coffee and pack my daughter's lunch. There were many mornings I turned Philippians 4:13 into a song, and I sang as I spread peanut butter and jelly on two slices of bread for my daughter's lunch. The words "I can do all things through Christ who gives me strength" became my theme song. Single moms, when you are weary and frustrated, start singing praises. Start speaking Scripture out loud. Turn your favorite verse into a song. You will be amazed at the difference it makes. The enemy who attacks our mind and wants to work through our emotions will flee when he hears praise and the Word. He can't stand it. Because where there is praise, there is God's spirit, and the Devil will not be in the same place where God's spirit dwells.

TEN THINGS TO REMEMBER AS A SINGLE MOM

If you are a single mom, there are some things I want you to always remember. Remind yourself of these things often!

1. Surrender.

When you surrender your life and your home to God and ask

Him to cover it, He will.

2. Allow Him to ordain your steps and your children's steps.
When you offer up your children to Him and decide to teach and train them for His kingdom, He will ordain your steps and lead you in the ways you should teach them.

3. Persevere.
When you persevere because your children are counting on you to be strong, He will give you supernatural strength. You may have only a loaf of bread and a can of beans in your cabinet, but trust in your Father who is taking care of you, and show your children how you trust. Show your kids how you rely on Christ to provide for you. Faith is so hard because it is hoping for what is not seen, but Jesus will meet your needs! If you don't feel like you have faith right now, find a way to fake it till your make it because you are their world, and if you fall apart, so will they. Even if you are trying to have faith, let them see that.

4. Always be easy on yourself![16]
Let's face it: You're doing alone what was designed to be a two-person job. The fact that you often feel physically, emotionally, and spiritually worn out is *not* just your imagination. But because your kids depend on you, you can't afford to push yourself past a certain point. You must take care of yourself and your health in order to be there for them.

Do not beat yourself up for all the things that you feel you should have done. Do the best you can for the day at hand, and know tomorrow is another day. Find ways to take a breather, even if you have to swap out childcare with another single parent to make it happen. Spend that time recharging in some way that will continue to pay benefits when the busyness kicks back in: with exercise, spiritual growth, or good, old-fashioned sleep. Take a look at these quick and easy energy boosters for ideas! It's not selfish to maintain the engine that keeps your home running: you.

5. Savor the season and keep on sowing.
In those moments when the kids are screaming and fighting, when they are struggling in school and it is only you at night to

help them, when you are tucking them in to bed at night, and then you finally land in your bed exhausted, keep telling yourself, "This too shall pass. There is a reason in this season. Jesus, help me to savor the season and keep on sowing into my children."

6. Conquer the battle in your mind.

Your mindset and your thought life will operate you. Don't throw pity parties. The enemy will use self-pity to keep you down. Speak the word out loud over your struggles, and make yourself have the right mindset. Align your mind, Sister, before it gets away from you. The right perspective and mindset will empower you.

7. You can only control yourself.

While you can't control others (like an ex-spouse), you can control your own decisions and get organized and intentional about how you handle your money to lessen the stress. Consult with a financial planner, or take a course at your church like Dave Ramsey's Financial Peace University to help make every dollar go as far as possible. Don't be ashamed to ask the church for help too. And remember: what your children need most is your love—and you do have that in abundance.

Lavish them with love, and lay down the guilt of not being able to give them every material thing they desire. When they are older, they won't remember what you bought them. They will remember most how loved they felt.

8. Do not socially isolate.

Single moms tell me that they sometimes feel trapped underneath a mountain of responsibility that never allows them to invest in friendships, much less find another companion for life. Some working single moms say the guilt of leaving their kids in the evening to do something just for themselves is crushing. Add to that the cost of hiring a sitter, and getting out of the house for adult interaction seems almost impossible.

You need friendships and encouragement. You need a community of people you can turn to. Look for environments that allow for some social time for you while your kids are being occupied or entertained: a church small group that offers childcare, an exercise class at a gym with a kids' space, or a play date with other parents. And maybe once a month, splurge for that sitter or trade out childcare with another parent to actually go to dinner with friends and really talk about what's going on in your life.

When I felt that my church didn't really have a place for single moms, I started a small group in my home. The moms brought their kids, and we all brought a dollar to pay my teenage neighbor to entertain them for an hour while we fellowshiped. We had a book study using a book about motherhood, and we also discussed ways we could turn to Christ in our struggles. We prayed for one another and lifted each other up. Then at times we all came together and played a game or did crafts. We had some awesome times of fellowship, and I was able to establish a community of friends with common struggles. There were times we watched each other's kids and had play dates so the moms could hang out too.

9. Get rid of guilt.[17]

Is there any end to the guilt a single parent feels? If you know that your decisions (some of which you may regret) contributed to your current family status, it's especially present. There's guilt about the financial things you can't provide, guilt about the time you spend away from them, guilt about the things you just can't do because of your situation. Regardless of how your children became the kids of a single parent, you worry daily about the effect that it's having on them and feel responsible.

If your single status is the result of a poor decision, own your mistake, learn from it, and move on. We all make mistakes, and the guilt we feel is only helpful inasmuch as it helps us to correct problems and become better people. Stop feeling guilty. Self-condemnation is a door the enemy could open wider and create a stronghold. God sees you through eyes of grace. You must try to see yourself through His eyes.

I often felt guilty for my choice to leave my children's father. I grieved when they would say they wished they were like other kids. Guilt swelled up in me many times, but I would also remind myself that the alternative would have been worse and more damaging. Ladies, if you left a relationship because it was more than you could bear, or because you knew that oppression would keep you from being a healthy person internally, your decision to save yourself so you could be a good mom to your kids is nothing to feel guilty over.

If your current situation is the result of the mistakes of another, do yourself a favor and forgive if you haven't already. The burden of anger is too much for you to bear, and bitterness will keep you from experiencing the freedom and peace you need. You can't get in a time machine and fix the past, but you can do your best to make today better—so focus your energy there. Work on relationships with your kids' other parent/stepparent so that they feel less friction. Be a great example today and trust God to fill in the gaps that are beyond your reach.

10. Create a community.

It grieves me that single moms seem to be the overlooked subgroup in a lot of churches, and because of this, a lot of single moms feel like they don't belong in churches. If you feel this way, please do not let this keep you from finding a church to belong to and get plugged into. As a single mom, you need a church community. Find a church that does home groups/life groups and if you can't find one you want to go to, start one! Don't feel like you have to be a spiritual leader to do this. Make it a book study. Learn and grow together.

If anyone needs a support group, it is single moms. So if you feel your church doesn't do much to reach out to single moms, then become the change you want to see! Go talk to some leaders in the church. Share your vision and see how they can support you. Perhaps they will be willing to offer the childcare and their facilities to have the meetings.

As hard as it is, there will be a day when you look back and say, "Wow, time has flown. I wish I had some of those years back when they were young." I look at my ten- and thirteen-year-old now and wish that.

Single moms, if you rely on Him and seek Him, He will give you the grace and strength you need to keep sowing into their lives, even when you feel no one is sowing into yours.

My best advice is this: This too shall pass. This valuable season may seem long, but one day when it is over, you want to be able to look back and feel proud and without regrets. Do not stop telling yourself you are awesome. You can stand up in the midst of your situation and feel empowered because your heavenly Husband has you (Isaiah 54:5).

CHAPTER 16: SINGLE MOMS EMPOWERED! REFLECTION QUESTIONS:

1. The life of a single mom is challenging but also rewarding beyond measure. When it comes to time management, you only have 24 hours in a day, but creating a morning and evening routine can benefit everyone in your household! Below, write out your morning routine from the time you wake up to the time you either get to work or drop your child off at school. If you don't have a routine, now is a great time to create one!

2. Now do the same for your afternoon and evening routines from the time your children come home until you go to bed.

a. As you review these routines, do you have any time set aside *just for you*? Do you have time to journal, pray, unwind, or read? If you don't do that on a regular basis, where can you find even five minutes for yourself each day?

3. Yes, you are a superhero! But you don't have to do everything by yourself. In the section titled "Ten Things to Remember as a Single Mom," the last item listed encourages you to create a community. Below, list members of your personal community, including church, friends, family, and your child's teachers. If you complete this exercise and still feel like you don't have enough people in your corner, this is your time to expand your community! Once you have made this list, find time to reach out to these important people once in a while, and don't be afraid to ask for help. For example: If your car breaks down and you don't have the money to fix it, call the church and ask if there are any men who can work on cars.

a. Make a list of three people, organizations, or groups that you can connect with in the next month.

17
Seeking a Holy Wholeness

We are destroying sophisticated arguments and
every exalted and proud thing that sets itself up against
the [true] knowledge of God, and we are taking every thought and
purpose captive to the obedience of Christ.
(2 CORINTHIANS 10:5 AMP)

When I finally did U-turn in my walk with Christ and in my choices, I knew at the time I was not whole. I didn't even understand what being whole totally looked like. I had heard the sermons before where preachers were telling me to be whole in Christ, but I didn't really know what that meant. So in my pursuit to work on myself, I set out to discover what it meant to be whole and how to get there.

WHAT DOES IT MEAN TO BE WHOLE?

We hear the word *wholeness* discussed in churches and books, but do you really know what it means to be a whole person? Preachers and counselors will tell you, and even I mentioned it in another chapter, that if you want a healthy, whole relationship, you have to become a whole person first. Becoming whole is a process that can sometimes take half a lifetime. But the important thing is to be *working on* being a whole person.

Some people are running from themselves. They simply don't want to stop and face the internal giants that are working as a force inside of them to affect many areas of life. It can be downright uncomfortable to take the time and effort to recognize we have issues that have to be dealt with and healed before we can get to another level in our lives. If you don't take the time while you are single to get to know who you are through self-reflection, and to identify what your issues may be, you will carry those issues into every relationship, including marriage.

Self-awareness is the first step on the road to wholeness, and there is no better time than while you are single to work on yourself. That is why I mentioned before that this season of singleness is a valuable time when you can become the best you through self-reflection and working on the things inside of you that need healing or changing.

A BIBLICAL VIEW ON WHOLENESS

When a manufacturer creates something, they expect it to perform and operate as they designed it. When the item is first created, it works perfectly, but over the course of being used by consumers, it begins to wear down and lose its sharpness and newness. If the object is mistreated and abused, it could possibly lose its functioning purpose altogether.

God designed us to be perfect, to be in His image. God is a leading force in this universe, and He also created us to be leaders with a destiny to lead in some aspect (Genesis 1:26–28; 2:19). When He looks at us, He sees us as the perfect image in His likeness that He created. We are tainted by sin and circumstances, but God always sees us through eyes of mercy and the *original* product He created to be perfect. When He made us, we were whole human beings. But over time, our wholeness is blocked or damaged by others, by situations, by sin, and by lack of spiritual maturity.

So is it possible to get back to that state of wholeness that God originally designed us for? A state where we are complete, reliant upon Him, and walking in spiritual maturity that leads to contentment? Yes, it is possible, but it takes your striving for it.

Matthew 5:48 says, "You, therefore, will be perfect . . . as your heavenly Father is perfect" (AMP).

Jesus longs for us to go through a process of perfection. You may be thinking right now that no one is perfect and ever will be but Jesus. That is true, but being perfect in a biblical perspective is very different than what we think in the natural sense. The perfection that Jesus speaks of in Matthew 5:48 is about having the spiritual maturity and self-discipline to function as the person God created us to be, while grace fills in the gaps. I love The Message Bible because the author put the Scripture in such a relatable way. Philippians 3:12–14 tells us that Paul had the concept of being whole in Christ figured out.

I'm not saying that I have this all together, and I have it made.
But I am well on my way, reaching out for Christ, who has so
wondrously reached out for me.
Friends, don't get me wrong:
By no means do I count myself an expert in all of this,
but I've got my eye on the goal,
where God is beckoning us onward—to Jesus.
I'm off and running, and I'm not turning back.
(PHILIPPIANS 3:12–14 MSG)

What is that goal that God was beckoning Paul and us to? It is the goal of being complete and mature in Him. So here are six steps that I discovered about being whole and what it looks like.

1. Understand what makes you *you*.

Understand that you have a body (flesh, the senses), spirit (the part God regenerates through salvation), and soul (the heart, emotions, intellect, will), and all three need to be properly nourished and maintained.

2. Become a mature believer.

As you nourish your spirit through God's Word and a relationship with Him, you mature in Christ. As you grow in Christ and in wisdom, there are three main areas we mature in:

a. How we relate to God: "And Jesus replied to him, 'You shall love the Lord your God with all your heart, and with all your soul, and with all your mind'" (Matthew 22:37 AMP). In The Message version of these verses, Jesus said, "Love the Lord your God with all your passion and prayer and intelligence." Going to church and hearing the Word preached does not bring about a relationship with Christ. Through prayer and private devotional time spent, "being still and knowing He is God" while we privately seek Him, we develop a relationship with Him that brings about wholeness. It is hard for some people to grasp the concept of a relationship with Jesus when we can't see Him or hear Him, but He will speak in our spirits when we are listening. It is faith combined with the Holy Spirit in you that deepens your understanding and relationship with Christ.

b. How we relate to ourselves: "I am wonderfully made" (Psalm 139:14). "God created me for a purpose" (Jeremiah 29:11). "God is our father" (2 Corinthians 6:17–18). "I'm a new creature" (2 Corinthians 5:17). "I am the righteousness of God through Jesus" (Romans 3:20–24). We mature in Christ and get closer to wholeness when we learn how to receive God's grace and love for us. When we grow in our relationship with Christ and our understanding of who He is, we can see the position we have in Him: a greatly treasured daughter of the most high God.

c. How we relate to others: "Love your neighbor as yourself [that is, unselfishly seek the best or higher good for others]" (Matthew 22:39). The Message version says, "Love others as well as you love yourself." When we mature in Christ and grow closer to wholeness, we should also mature in how we think when it comes to relating to others. Because the Holy Spirit is in us when we become Christians, the fruits of the Spirit are also in us. The fruits of the Spirit are listed in Galatians 5:22–23: "But the fruit of the Spirit is love, joy, peace, forbearance, kindness, goodness, faithfulness, gentleness and self-control" (NIV). So as we mature in Christ, we should also be able to relate to others with a greater measure of the fruits of the Spirit.

Are we kind? Are we patient with others? Do we promote peace in situations more than we promote conflict and strife? Do we try to have self-control when it comes to situations that cause anger, or do we just have self-control over how we choose to conduct our lives? When we grow in our relationship with the Lord, we should be producing more "fruitful" acts. No one is perfect in this area, but what matters most is that we don't give up in growing spiritual fruit—which in essence is mannerisms, character traits, and actions we display toward ourselves and others that we know Christ wants us to have.

3. Have a mature and controlled thought life.

I've mentioned this several times because we can conquer so many areas we struggle with in life once we conquer controlling our thoughts. Our thought life matters!

Taking control of our thoughts and choosing to use God's Word in every situation is a sure sign of a mature thought life. The key to having the healthiest life is understanding that, like it or not, you are in a war—one that you didn't ask for. Your presence on this earth is a threat to the kingdom of darkness.

As believers, we are not exempt from uncomfortable and negative experiences. In fact, the Bible says it rains on the just as well as the unjust. Your responses to these experiences, as well as the outcomes, can ultimately be traced to your thought life. We have to know that we can't simply accept everything that pops into our mind. Sometimes our natural thoughts contradict the Word of God, therefore, we have to check and rein in all of our thoughts.

4. Ask Jesus to heal your past.

Christ wants us to be healed. God wants us to be made whole! As it says in Colossians 1:13–14, "For he has rescued us out of the darkness and gloom of Satan's kingdom and brought us into the Kingdom of His dear Son, who bought our freedom with his blood and forgave us all our sins" (TLB). Trust in Christ and pray for inner healing so that you can walk in the freedom and not in "heavy heartedness," feeling as though you're burdened with a heavy life.

5. Guard your heart!

Does our heart really have feelings? We say, "He broke my heart," or "Guard your heart," but our heart is just a muscle that pumps blood. Without our hearts doing the functions that it does, we would surely die. The Bible mentions the heart several times: "Out of the heart flows" . . . "Love with all your heart." But since our heart controls our life, why don't we just replace the word *heart* with *life*?

When we guard our hearts, we are really in essence guarding our life. We should guard who and what we allow in our life, where we allow our life to go, and what we allow our life to focus on and commit to. One aspect of being whole and mature in Christ is guarding your actions and what you do with your heart: your life.

Watch over your heart [life] with all diligence, for from it flow the springs of life. Put away from you a deceitful (lying, misleading) mouth, and put devious lips far from you. Let your eyes look directly ahead [toward the path of moral courage] and let your gaze be fixed straight in front of you [toward the path of integrity]. Consider well and watch carefully the path of your feet, and all your ways will be steadfast and sure.
Do not turn away to the right
nor to the left [where evil may lurk];
turn your foot from [the path of] evil.
(PROVERBS 4:23–27 AMP)

6. Keep your attitude in check.

Your attitude is critical when building a successful mindset and controlled thought life. The Bible is filled with examples of proper attitudes of mature believers.

"Blessed [spiritually prosperous, happy, to be admired] are the poor in spirit [those devoid of spiritual arrogance, those who regard themselves as insignificant], for theirs is the kingdom of heaven [both now and forever]. Blessed [forgiven, refreshed by God's grace] are those who mourn [over their sins and repent], for

*they will be comforted [when the burden of sin is lifted]. Blessed
[inwardly peaceful, spiritually secure, worthy of respect] are the
gentle [the kind-hearted, the sweet-spirited, the self-controlled],
for they will inherit the earth. Blessed [joyful, nourished by God's
goodness] are those who hunger and thirst for righteousness [those
who actively seek right standing with God], for they will be [com-
pletely] satisfied. Blessed [content, sheltered by God's promises]
are the merciful, for they will receive mercy. Blessed [anticipating
God's presence, spiritually mature] are the pure in heart [those
with integrity, moral courage, and godly character], for they will
see God. Blessed [spiritually calm with life-joy in God's favor] are
the makers and maintainers of peace, for they will [express His
character and] be called the sons of God. Blessed [comforted by
inner peace and God's love] are those who are persecuted for doing that which is morally right, for theirs is the kingdom of heaven
[both now and forever]."*
(MATTHEW 5:3–10 AMP)

We are blessed and feel whole when we can have a good attitude, one that tries to reflect the character of Christ.

Becoming whole is a process and takes focused effort and
consciousness. We have to become reliant upon Christ to be our
all and take the steps to be whole and mature in Christ. We all fall
short of displaying these fruits and having a Christlike attitude
all of the time. But the most important thing when it comes to
becoming whole and mature in Christ is that we don't give up in
moving forward. We don't give up growing through grace when
we make mistakes in our actions and attitude. Christ longs for us
to be whole and complete in Him; reliant upon Him to meet our
every need and fill us with strength and joy. He will never stop
helping us achieve wholeness when we seek it.

CHAPTER 17: SEEKING A HOLY WHOLENESS
REFLECTION QUESTIONS:

1. Even though man is born into sin, God designed us to be perfect and when He looks at us, He sees us as the perfect image in

His likeness that He created. We have a body (flesh, the senses), Spirit (the part God regenerates through salvation), and Soul (the heart, emotions, intellect, will), and all three need to be nourished and maintained. Below, list several ways that you nourish each part of you.

a. I nourish my body by…

b. I nourish my spirit by…

c. I nourish my soul by…

2. If you don't nourish these parts of yourself regularly, list at least two ways that you can begin doing so for each part— body, spirit, and soul.

3. What is your definition of a mature Christian? Are there ways you feel you can mature and grow in Christ?

4. None of us is perfect when it comes to possessing or behaving with the fruits of the spirit, as discussed in Galatians 5:22.

a. What fruits of the spirit do you need to work on perfecting?

b. List ways you can perfect those qualities (fruits) in yourself.

18
Get Back Up

*But He said to me, "My grace is sufficient for you,
for my power is made perfect in weakness."
Therefore I will boast all the more gladly about my weaknesses, so
that Christ's power may rest on me.*
(2 CORINTHIANS 12:9 NIV)

It took me a while to learn that happiness (Jesus joy) and contentment is a choice and a forced mindset. To find contentment, I had to choose what I was going to believe about myself and speak over my own life. We only truly find contentment when we begin to change on the inside and when we are ready to make a mental shift. We have to stand up and choose to mentally live in the present and refuse to dwell on the past. We have to stop looking back at our past and press forward.

It is so easy to put labels on our own lives. I still struggle with this, but when I catch myself doing it, I choose to believe God's Word over what my emotions want to tell me. I make mistakes in my walk with Christ where I act outside of the mind of Christ, but is any other human being any different? When we make mistakes; we just have to learn from them and move on.

"Don't be stuck in a rut of yesterday's loss and disappointments. The word says that we have to forget what is behind and press for-

ward. You can't change your yesterdays but you can change who you are and what you are becoming now and tomorrow."
—T. D. JAKES

I used to beat myself up over my failures until I realized that was also keeping me from feeling content. If you are living your life the best you can live, but you sin or make a mistake, go to God and then get up and go forward. If you make a mistake in your dating life or any other area, before you move into a guilt mode, understand that your sin attracts God's grace. God's grace is never to be taken for granted and used as a pass for sin, but Romans 5:21 says, "Grace takes the weight off of our regret."

God's law was given so that all people could see how sinful they were. But as people sinned more and more, God's wonderful grace became more abundant. So just as sin ruled over all people and brought them to death, now God's wonderful grace rules instead, giving us right standing with God and resulting in eternal life through Jesus Christ our Lord.
(ROMANS 5:20–21 NLT)

When you reach a point in your single life where you are charging full speed ahead at pursuing a vision, even when you are experiencing true joy and fulfillment, there will eventually be a setback. That's just life. It could be a setback from a dating experience, a job loss, a financial loss, etc. We just cannot let ourselves sit down in defeat when we face a setback.

Sometimes we go to amazing church services and feel pumped up by the Word and choose a new mindset at the end of the sermon. Then Monday morning comes and work challenges and life disappointments come throughout the week, and we quickly start to find our way back to a rut.

As I mentioned in chapter 12, Aligning Your Mind, we have to choose how we see our circumstances. Do not choose to wear the negative-stained glasses the enemy constantly tries to force on your head. The enemy may momentarily knock you down, or you may knock your own self down from bad choices, but get back up. No one ever fulfills a vision or purpose by staying down. You have to keep pressing on.

I press on toward the goal to win the prize [the answer to the dream and vision] for which God has called me heavenward in Christ Jesus.
(PHILIPPIANS 3:14 NIV)

Sometimes we have to silence the negative voices of others in order to move forward. If you have people around you negatively influencing you, silence them. Remove yourself if you have to. You will never advance into your God-given purpose when you have others speaking negativity into your life. Surround yourself with people who will speak *life* into your life.

When you face failures and setbacks, embrace them as part of a plan, and pick yourself back up and move forward. Stay on the road you know Jesus wants you on, even though you have no idea where it leads. God has a way of bringing greatness out of pain. He will birth strength in weakness, and He will call something forth through failure and pain.

We grow from failure because adversity produces growth. Failure has a way of making us unsatisfied with where we are and making us plead to go to the next level. So do not beat yourself up over failures. If you do, it will certainly make it hard for you to feel content or to forgive yourself. Never forget that God's grace is always sufficient no matter how large we feel the failure is. Just because we make mistakes, and areas of our lives are not functioning the way we want them to function, it does not mean there is not grace and favor still in place.

When you face failures that you feel are setbacks, learn from them, accept His grace, and give yourself grace. Do not take steps backward after falling down. That is just what Satan wants you to do. When we stay in a rut after experiencing a setback, we are allowing Satan to have victory.

CHAPTER 18: GET BACK UP
REFLECTION QUESTIONS:

1. Happiness is a choice. Sometimes we have to keep making that choice daily...even hourly! But it is worth the effort. Sometimes it helps to surround ourselves with reminders of things that make us happy! List eight things below (they can be smells, sounds, pictures, locations, animals, people, etc.) that automatically put you in a good mood.

    a. How many of those items do you have in your home or workspace?

    b. Just as a vision board is a visual reminder of your goals, having happy items throughout your home and workplace can relieve stress, promote relaxation, and give you a mental break amid chaotic moments. If you don't currently have any of these items on hand, try to incorporate them into your life this week!

2. In chapter 12 we talked about aligning our minds with scripture to help pick us back up when we're down. Find some verses in the scripture section at the end of the book or in the Bible

that will lift you up when you feel you have made a mistake, and write them below.

3. Another way to overcome adversity or feelings of failure is to find the positive in the midst of pain or regret. Below, list four benefits that are gained by overcoming adversity and mistakes.

19

A Happy Ending to a New Beginning

However, as it is written: "What no eye has seen, what no ear has heard, and what no human mind has conceived"—the things God has prepared for those who love Him.
(1 CORINTHIANS 2:9 NIV)

When I became focused on personal growth and finding a purpose for God, I no longer had any expectations of meeting someone. I was content and resigned to the fact that I might be a single mom until my kids were grown, and I was okay with that if that was God's plan for my life. I told God many times that if He wanted me to have someone, He would have to bring him right in front of me because I was no longer looking, noticing, or searching. I made up my mind that in this season of my life, I would find joy and happiness in my Lord and in pouring into the lives of my children and others. I served in the children's ministry at my church and got involved in more life groups. I refused to wear any stereotyping labels that society often gives, such as "divorced single mom," as if that is something to be pitied or looked down upon. That was my situation, but that was not who I was. I know that God can use anyone and anything regardless of their situation.

I wrestled with God prompting me to write a book. I battled

with insecurities, and Satan constantly told me I was not qualified. But I knew that if God could use a burning bush to get His message out and even speak through a donkey, He could certainly speak through me. I kept reminding myself that God does not call the qualified, He qualifies the called. If you have a story of how you have overcome a trial and God has gotten the victory, write it out and share it! Our trials become our testimony. We glorify God when we share our testimony.

After hearing a sermon on vision and purpose, I told myself I would no longer wait until my marital status changed. I established a vision for my life as a single woman. I wanted to help other young single women, as well as single moms, find contentment in Christ and not make mistakes like I did out of fear and settling. My vision became writing a book that could help others avoid traps planted by the enemy but would also help them move beyond a past that the enemy tries to use to keep them in bondage.

So while I was finally busy living (and enjoying!) my single life, to my surprise and totally unexpectedly, God brought a man across my path that I would have never chosen in my own searching. I would have passed him by in an Internet dating search. I probably would have said no to a friend who wanted to set me up with him because he is not the kind of man I would have fallen for, had I been looking through my "ideal man glasses." I am so glad God had His own ideal for me. When I got to know my now-husband, I began to see his heart, and I realized he was exactly what God knew I needed. And he had been right in front of me for a year.

RIGHT IN FRONT OF ME

To this day, I still marvel over the fact that I spent one night a week for a year in the same room with my now-husband, and I *never even noticed him.* I was even more surprised when I found out that he played keyboard on the praise and worship team twice a month at the church I had attended for the last two years, but I *had never seen him!*

Maybe because he did not fit the profile of what I thought I wanted, God kept us from noticing each other or meeting because it wasn't time. There was still a work He was doing inside of both of us. Prior to our meeting, he was still healing and getting his life organized after the ending of a sixteen-year marriage that he could no longer endure. While he was healing, I was on a road to finding wholeness in Christ. Had we met any earlier, we would not have been whole individuals capable of having a strong, Christ-centered marriage.

The man God finally brought into my life supports me and believes in me like no one I ever met before. He pushes me and challenges me to reach my goals, and no other person I met before treated me in such a supportive way.

BUT FIRST . . .

Before I continue my story of how we met, I want to add that I do not condone divorce. I believe God hates divorce and it wrecks the lives of children the most. Divorce should never be an option unless a couple has tried everything and it gets to a point where neither person can be the person they need to be because they are under too much oppression from the marriage, or if there is abuse. There is no doubt that God can change hearts and heal broken marriages. I do not think anyone should give up on a marriage unless they have tried all they can. A marriage takes two people to make it strong. One spouse cannot heal it and strengthen it alone.

Oftentimes when we are young, we marry in our own will based on emotions and what we believe is best, but it isn't a marriage in God's will for us. A marriage that God never intended for us will struggle. He can still bless it and make something good come from it, but both people have to have a certain mindset. We serve a God of second chances, a merciful God. Sometimes we take the wrong road, but when we are ready to make a U-turn and pursue His will for our lives, He will open doors we never imagined.

If you are reading this as a divorced woman, do not allow

Satan to tell you that God is angry at you or that you are finished when it comes to pleasing Him and fulfilling a purpose. God is not disappointed in you. Do not wear a self-inflicted scarlet letter because you are divorced. Churches preach that God can't stand divorce, but if you chose divorce or your spouse forced it, do not ever think that your situation is causing God to remove His favor from your life. He knew your life and the paths you would follow when you were conceived. He *already* established a road for your life named *purpose* and *destiny* beyond relationships that end.

God's Word says He will work all things for your good because He is going to do a new thing. Your past situations may have led you to dry wastelands of pain (Isaiah 43:19), shame, and regret, but our God doesn't leave you where you have been. He has prepared something for you that you cannot even imagine.

THE ORCHESTRATION

One evening I took my son to his school for a weekly Cub Scout meeting. While I was in the teachers' lounge grading papers, a gentleman came in to get a soda from the machine, and we started a conversation. We were surprised to learn that we went to the same church of about one thousand people in any given service, but neither of us recognized each other from church. It did not take me long in talking to this man to see the love of God radiating from his gentle demeanor. I didn't even check out his ring finger or ask his marital status. My only impression was that he was a very nice man.

Over the course of the next four months, we spoke at the scout meetings and developed a friendship. I noticed he came alone and did not wear a ring, so that is when I asked about his personal life out of curiosity. He shared with me the struggles of going through a divorce, and we began to share how our walks with God carried us through our difficult times and helped us to forgive.

There was not a huge attraction on my end in the first month I knew him. He did not fit the image of what I had in my mind for "my type." Over the next four months, we built a friendship at Cub Scouts and at church. As I watched him play keyboard at church, and saw the talent and heart for worship he has, I slowly began to develop an interest in him due to the personality and demeanor I saw in him.

After those four months of getting to know each other, we began spending time together, and it grew from there. *I fell for him from the inside out.* I knew he was the real deal and a true man of God. I knew that because he didn't just talk the talk. His love for God radiated through his demeanor and talents.

Had I seen my husband's profile on a dating website, I would have passed him by. On the outside, he did not fit the "ideal" that I was looking for, mainly because of his race. Our society has trained our minds and views of man's skin tone, but skin is nothing more than a shell to hold the soul and mind. When God sees us, He sees our soul, not our skin. The character, mind, and soul are what make a man. Not his skin. Love should never know a boundary, especially one as minuscule as race. Before I met my husband, I did not always have that open mindset when it came to dating, but once again I say that God was still preparing me and making me into the woman He needed me to be for my future.

I mentioned that he wasn't what I thought I wanted, but God knew all along that he is exactly what I need. I am so thankful our ways are not God's ways, because I do not think I could ever find a man as special and as rare as my husband on a dating website. We write together, worship and pray together, have goals together, talk about the Word together, and have Bible studies. Every Sunday when I watch him lead a congregation and worship team into praise, I thank God He finally answered my prayers for what I always longed for.

After celebrating our one-year anniversary, I can honestly say I know what it is like to have a soul mate. I can't imagine another person being more perfect for me. We do not have a ministry together like I always wanted, but I know that is yet to come.

Ladies, God knows what you need better than you even know yourself. I want to encourage you to lay down your own checklist and ideals for what you want in a man, and trust that God will bring you what is best for your personality and for your purpose.

You never know. He may have been standing in front of you all along.

CHAPTER 19: A HAPPY ENDING TO A NEW BEGINNING
REFLECTION QUESTIONS:

1. We've all heard of "happily ever after" stories. We may even have parents or grandparents who have picture-perfect marriages. Their stories give us hope that we will find our soul mate one day. Think about the people in your life who have great relationships. Below, list two couples and explain why you admire their relationship. If you do not know how they met, ask them.

2. Many of us have a "type" when it comes to dating and while there's nothing necessarily wrong with having physical preferences that we find attractive, we might be overlooking a great guy in our midst because he doesn't fit our type.
   a. What is your "type"? List your physical, social, and cultural preferences.

b. Of those items listed, is each one necessary to your happiness? Chances are if you really think about your list of preferences, some of them are only there out of habit and based on the types of men you've dated in the past. Below, which item(s) could you remove from your "must have" list?

c. What kind of man *do you think you need*? Write it below if you have figured it out. Since God knows what we need more than we do, pray and ask God to bring you what He knows what you need when it is His best time for you both.

20
Pursue Your Purpose

"For we are His workmanship, created in
Christ Jesus for good works, which God prepared
beforehand that we should walk in them."
(EPHESIANS 2:10 NKJV)

The purpose of something is the reason it is created. Its destiny is where it is going to end up. Don't waste valuable time with people who do not contribute to your growth, vision, and destiny, and don't delay your destiny by making bad choices.

We all want our lives to count for something. We feel more fulfilled when we do something that we know makes a difference in some arena. Our goal may be to be the best we can be in our careers, to achieve wealth, to make an impact in the lives of others, or to have our own business. The list goes on. I think a majority of people want to know they serve a purpose, to stand for something and make a difference somewhere.

Some people get destiny and purpose mixed up. Purpose is something you do. It is using your talents to be of service to others. Destiny is where God ultimately takes you as a result of what you do within your purpose. It is my belief that we can serve many purposes as we go through seasons of our life, and those purposes mold us to fulfill a destiny. As we surrender to God and serve Him within a purpose, He develops us for our destiny.

One of the most inspirational women on the planet is Joyce Meyers. She had a bad childhood, but she overcame her wounds and turned her trials into a testimony. She did not wait around, thinking she was too damaged to help others. At the age of thirty-two, she began leading a Bible study in her home. The Bible study grew into church facilities, and ten years later, she began Joyce Meyers Ministries.

Do you think during those ten long years of using her gifts with a purpose in home and church Bible studies that she knew she would one day have an international ministry? No. She may have hoped for it, but it has gone beyond more than she ever imagined it would. At thirty-two, she knew she had the gift to teach, but she didn't know her destiny was an international ministry. She stepped out and began to serve a purpose and use her God-given talents. Her purpose for ten years was to minister to people in her sphere of influence. As she walked in a purpose of serving and using her gifts, God developed her gifts and created the path for her future. He ordered her steps into what He knew He had for her.

GETTING RID OF THE ROADBLOCK

To this day, I can't tell you why Jesus allowed me to see Him at the age of nine in that near-death experience, but I am so thankful He did. That experience allowed me to hold on to the belief that God had not given up on me due to my failures and mistakes. Satan had done such a number on me with self-condemnation, but my experience at age nine was the "thread" that kept me hanging on to the hope that I could still make a difference for God and in the life of another.

Until the age of thirty-six, I spent my entire adult life thinking that I would find the special destiny God had spoken over me in the bright light after the car crash *once I got married.* I thought for so long that it would be my husband who had a ministry, and I would be his helpmate and help him in his ministry.

When I stopped allowing Satan to hold me down due to a life status (being single) and made the choice to step out in faith and use a gift God had placed in me, I discovered a godly confidence that I had never known. I began to realize that God never tells us or desires for us to wait until we have "arrived" at a certain position in life. We can be His hands and feet and spread a message anytime and anyplace, regardless of what status and credentials we have.

I am so thankful that after twelve years of detours, I finally made a U-turn in my single life and decided to wait on God's timing and His ways, while I stepped out of my own insecurities and allowed Him to use me. I had made up my mind that I would create a fabulous single life and stop waiting on my circumstances to change. I was going to pursue my dreams and heart's desire myself. I found a purpose in my present state of life and gave it my best. I stopped allowing myself to be my own roadblock; I had done that too long. After making a U-turn in the Single Lane of settling and disappointment I was on, I established a vision for my life as a single woman and pursued it.

The Word says that where there is no vision, the people will perish (Proverbs 29:18). My vision became that of helping other women, who felt broken from a bad past, to find healing and wholeness in Christ and overcome the bondage the enemy wants to keep us in. I was not going to delay something that God had put on my heart because of my marital status, my financial status, my past, or my classification in society: a divorced single mom. I started a single moms' life group, and my purpose during that season of my life was to encourage and start a network of support for them.

You don't need an encounter with Jesus to believe that He has many special purposes for your life, purposes that will lead to an amazing destiny. His Word already says He has plans to prosper you and do more than you can ever ask or imagine. So do not do as I did and disqualify yourself just because you have made some poor choices. You have a purpose to fulfill!

DON'T DELAY THE VISION

God has a vision for your life as a single woman. You are chosen and you are called. He gave you talents and abilities that only you can exercise in your way with your personality. Before you were born, God gave you a unique mixture of spiritual gifts, passions, abilities, personality, and experiences. There's no one like you in the entire universe because, in part, there's no one with your unique mix of talents. No one can do what you are able and willing to do exactly like you can. His vision for you has never changed from the time you were conceived, *but* God gives us a free will.

The vision that God has for our lives is not for us. It is a vision He has for how He can use us in the lives of others and to advance His kingdom. Being used by God does not have to be in some *grand* way such as preaching, singing, and writing books. Every act of kindness and extending God's love is walking in purpose.

In fact, you are used through purpose when you pray for a friend, when you give to the needy, when you encourage someone to lean on Jesus, when you go to church and serve in some aspect, when you feed the homeless, when you spread joy to the often forgotten in the nursing homes, when you teach Sunday school, and even when you share your testimony! The list goes on and on. Don't think that if your action doesn't equate to something big that it is not just as important. He longs for us to be His hands and feet on the earth and go anywhere there is need.

By our free will and bad choices, we may *delay* the destiny He has for us, but I want to assure you that it is never something that He takes away from us. Many people delay their destiny. In fact, it is possible to go through your entire life and miss God's destiny—by your own choices that may take you farther away from Him. If you choose to chase pleasure, popularity, money, and the wrong men instead of God, you'll miss it. And that is tragic. That is why the Word says that many are called but few are chosen (Matthew 22:14). Every child of God has a destiny. He calls everyone, but we have to pursue His calling by stepping out in purpose while we pursue a relationship with Him wholeheartedly.

God's will is not automatic, nor will He force it on you. He allows us to make choices. Many of the things that happen to you are not God's perfect will. We all have to choose between God's will and our own will. If I were to get drunk, fall in a pool, and drown, that wouldn't be God's will for my life. It would be due to my own stupid decision. I don't know about you, but I don't want to make stupid decisions anymore! I want to walk in that abundant life He says He wants me to have.

Here is the beautiful thing that I have seen happen in the lives of others and have experienced in my own life. Even when you mess up, God can turn disaster into a road to destiny. It's never too late to have His perfect will in your life. Just pray, "God, I want your purpose for my life," and you won't miss it, no matter where you've been. He'll get you in line with His purpose. He wants you to fulfill your destiny more than you do because it not for your benefit. It is for His.

Biblical destiny is this beautiful gift God gives to us, yet it is only realized as we walk in it God's way. We must realize that it is conditional based upon our response to God. Discovering the destiny and purpose God has for you is a process. The biggest part of the equation is *us*! God cannot walk us into a purpose to glorify His kingdom when we are running down the wrong road with the wrong mindset.

When you step out to fulfill a purpose, your steps will be ordered to your destiny, which may include the man you desire. You have no idea where God can take you and what He can orchestrate for you.

I still don't know what my final destiny is. I have a vision for where I hope God takes me, but for now I am following His leading and pursuing the purpose that I want to have by using the gifts He has given me.

As I pursued my purpose with a passion and tunnel vision on Christ, God brought the man I had always prayed for across my path. He now encourages me and supports me as I continue to pursue the vision I established when I was single. We have also begun to pursue a purpose together of writing and having a Bible study with friends.

BE A WOMAN OF FAITH

I love the story of Hannah in the Bible. It is one of God unfolding a master plan that she was not able to see during her years of waiting and longing. She was a married woman who had an adoring husband. She had everything she needed because she was wealthy, but the one thing she wanted the most, she wasn't able to have. She watched all the women around her having babies, and I imagine that in secret, she cried out to God, "Why not me?" People in ancient Israel believed that a large family was a blessing from God. Infertility, therefore, was a source of humiliation and shame. To make matters worse, her husband's other wife had not only bore him children but taunted Hannah mercilessly. Hannah was driven to prayer.

She cried out to God often. In one prayer where she uttered words to God while weeping, Eli heard her prayer and answered, "Go in peace, and may the God of Israel grant you what you have asked of him" (1 Samuel 1:17 NIV). After Hannah and her husband, Elkanah, returned from Shiloh to their home at Ramah, they slept together. Scripture says, "and the LORD remembered her" (1 Samuel 1:19 NIV). She became pregnant, had a son, and named him Samuel, which means "God hears."

But Hannah had made a promise to God that if she bore a son, she would give him back for God's service. Hannah followed through on that promise. She handed her young child Samuel over to Eli for training as a priest. God blessed Hannah further for honoring her pledge to Him. She bore three more sons and two daughters. Samuel grew up to become the last of Israel's judges, its first prophet, and counselor to its first two kings, Saul and David.[18]

Besides God giving her the desires of her heart in His timing, the part that encourages me is that God blessed Hanna *even more* when she honored God. Use this season of waiting to not only better yourself through personal growth, but to also take a step out in faith and use your talents for a purpose. Don't get weary in your waiting. No matter how long it may be, you have got to have faith that God sees the bigger picture and that his delays for your heart's desires are not to punish you. God has a plan, and that plan has a timeline.

Step out in faith, ladies. Don't let your talents lie dormant in you. Use them for the reason He gave them to you: to honor Him. When you establish a vision for your life and step out with the will to follow Him with reckless abandon, you will see how He will order your steps to blessings.

MAKE A U-TURN

Daughters of God, there is a road that God longs for you to travel. It is a road where you lay your own will and desires to the side and fall in love with Jesus in a way you have never known before. It is a road where you become mature in Christ and feel whole and complete in Him. It is a road where you forgive those who have hurt you and let go of the past that wants to keep you in a prison. It is a road where you are no longer led by your own emotions, but you are led by the Word of God and the Holy Spirit living in you. He wants to be the Lover of your soul, the one you find strength and contentment in. He wants to bless you and grant your heart's desires, but He also wants first place in your life. He longs for you to be whole so that you can have the maturity to walk forward into your destiny that He designed for you. His road is a road that leads to joy, fulfillment, and blessings.

Matthew 6:33 reminds us to "seek first the kingdom of God and His righteousness [His will], and all these things [your purpose, your desires, your destiny] shall be added to you" (NKJV). Use this valuable season of your life to become a more fabulous you as you pursue God's will. Put on your "faith-walking shoes" and walk down the road that leads to wholeness and purpose. While pursuing Jesus and a purpose in Him, you will be amazed at where He leads you.

Biblical destiny is a beautiful gift God gives to us, yet it is only realized *as we walk in it.* We have to realize that it is conditional based upon our response—our efforts to follow Him and pursue wholeness. Don't ever think you are not good enough to pursue His will and His purpose. Move forward knowing that God is doing a new thing. He changes you and equips you while you're on the journey!

Celebrate and pursue your purpose, Single Woman. Your purpose in this season is to be an amazing daughter of God who lacks nothing in Him. Your purpose is to turn your trials into testimony to bring Him glory. Your purpose is to pursue Him and discover the woman God says is fearfully and wonderfully made. Allow God to use you in ways you never dreamed or imagined. You are His masterpiece no matter where you have been or what has happened in your yesterdays. When He looks at you, He sees who He is molding you to be. Walk on, Sister. Walk tall in grace on the road that will lead you into what God designed you to be. This season can be fabulous because you are a fabulous single woman. How do I know this? Because God says you are!

CHAPTER 20: PURSUE YOUR PURPOSE
REFLECTION QUESTIONS:

1. God has a vision for your life, whether you're single or married. We may not know our ultimate purpose yet, but we can use our gifts every day to bring joy to our lives, as well as the lives of those around us. Below, list five gifts or talents you have, and don't be afraid to think outside the box! (Examples are singing, painting, managing multiple projects at once, teaching, writing, gardening, and fundraising.)

2. As we pursue our purpose and passions, we have less time to worry about being single. We also have an opportunity to grow our self-confidence, experience new things, and share our lives with people we would have otherwise never met. Below, list one thing you can do this week that will allow you to have a conversation with someone you've never met before, or else allow you to meet a need somewhere by using a talent you have.

3. There is a road that God longs for you to travel, and it might just require a U-turn. Are you ready to try dating His way instead of your way? If you're ready, I'm going to ask you to do some big things!

   a. First, take out your phone. Scroll through all of your contacts and delete the names and numbers of any men who no longer meet your new criteria. This should include any ex-boyfriends who tempt you to get back together for the wrong reasons. This also includes any men who do not have your best interest in mind and are only interested in getting to know you physically.

   b. Next, go through your social media accounts and use the same process. Unfollow or unfriend anyone who tempts you to fall back into old patterns.

   c. If you are currently using an online dating profile, use your new standards to evaluate each and every man you're in contact with. Don't worry if this eliminates 99% of the men. Remember, you're only looking for *one good man* anyway! You might also revise the wording on your profile to more clearly state who you are, who you are looking for, and why.

4. That's a lot of work already! Consider it clearing out the cobwebs and creating space for the right person to come into your life. The last step is really the most important—set your intention (and say it out loud) using God's Word as both the foundation and guide for your dating life from now on. Feel free to write your own declaration below or use this one:

"God, I acknowledge that Your ways are higher than my ways and You want the best for me. I desire to be in a great relationship that is blessed by You and I acknowledge that I need Your help. Until I meet that special person, help me to use my time wisely, help me to see my value and use my gifts, and gently nudge me when I veer off course. Thank You for Your grace, Your lovingkindness, and Your provision. In Jesus' name, Amen."

A Single Prayer

Father God, I come before You and lift up my praise to You. I thank You that Your mercy is new every morning and that You have called me a chosen one. Thank You for all the provisions You have made on my behalf and for protecting me from the snare of the enemy. Thank You for forgiving my fleshly weakness and my failures of the past. I praise You that there is no condemnation for those who are in You, Lord.

Your Word says in Isaiah 43:18 to "forget the former things" and not to dwell on the past, because You are doing a new thing in my life. You are making a way for me even when everything seems "dry" in my life. My past is under the blood. You do not see my past or my failures when You look at me. You see me as the perfect workmanship You created. I will not let my mistakes and failure of the past dictate who I am. I will believe in what You say that I am. You say I am redeemed, called by name, and that I am Yours.

I know sin is designed to destroy my life, and the enemy wants to form weapons against me to harm me, but I praise You, Lord, that You are my faith and shield and that no weapon formed against me will prosper. I may be pressed on all sides by trials, but I will not be crushed or driven to despair, because my hope is in You. I must capture my thoughts and align myself with Your Word to be the light You have called me to be. Help me, Lord, to come against the battle in my mind, and help me to stand against the one who wants to defeat me.

Lord, I thank You that You go before me and make the crooked paths straight (Isaiah 45:2). I do not see the future like You can, so I praise You for always working on my behalf even when I can't realize it or see it. Thank You for closing doors that I did not have the power to close and for opening doors in the past and in the future that would need to be opened.

Your Word tells me that I am precious to You, and because

You are my Father, You want what is best for me. Teach me to be patient as I wait for You to show me what is best. Help me to recognize the distractions Satan will try to put in my path to try and distract me from Your plans for me. You never default on Your Word and Your promises. Because Your Word says that You work all things for the good of those who love You, I trust that You are working through every season of my life.

I understand, Father, that I need to grow into an awesome woman of God before I can request an awesome man of God. I need to sharpen my spiritual gifts to the point that I am confident, strong, and packed with believing power. Then together, my future husband and I can stand firmly together, prepared and fully armed against the weapons of the enemy. So while I am patiently waiting and working toward being whole in You, I ask that every day You teach me those things that will help me to be the best that I can be. And when I am fully ready according to Your standard, if it is Your will, please present to me a godly man who will love me as Jesus Christ loves His Church.

As I grow in wholeness, Lord, I ask that You help me to recognize the gift and talent You have placed in me. Give me opportunities to serve so that I may begin to walk in a purpose that will lead me closer to the destiny that You have designed for me.

Only You, Lord, can fill my every need. I seek You now to be my heavenly Husband as Your Word says in Isaiah 54:5. Show me how I can be content in You as I embrace this season of life with thankfulness.

And I thank You, God, and praise You for how You have so magnificently blessed me. Even though I stand without a mate at this moment, I am not alone. You are surrounding me with favor like a shield (Psalm 5:12). You go before me, and You will never leave or forsake me (Deuteronomy 31:6).

Thank You, Lord, that You are the Puzzle Master of my life. Please help me to make good choices from here forward so that I do not distort the master plan You are unfolding. Teach me to walk in faith as I grow in You.

In Jesus' name. Amen.

Appendix: Power Scriptures to Use as a Sword

SCRIPTURE REGARDING FAITH

"I the Lord search the heart and test the mind, to give every man according to his ways, according to the fruit of his deeds." (JEREMIAH 17:10 ESV)

"Commit your work to the Lord, and your plans will be established." (PROVERBS 16:3 ESV)

"For whoever would save his life will lose it, but whoever loses his life for my sake will find it." (MATTHEW 16:25 ESV)

"When the righteous cry for help, the Lord hears and delivers them out of all their troubles." (PSALM 34:17 ESV)

"Trust in the Lord, and do good; so you will live in the land, and enjoy security. Take delight in the Lord, and he will give you the desires of your heart. Commit your way to the Lord; trust in him, and he will act. . . . Be still before the Lord, and wait patiently for him; . . ." (PSALM 37:3–5, 7A NRSV)

"Unless the Lord builds the house, those who build it labor in vain. Unless the Lord guards the city, the guard keeps watch in vain. It is in vain that you rise up early and go late to rest, eating the bread of anxious toil; for he gives sleep to his beloved." (PSALM 127:1–2 NRSV)

"Trust in the Lord with all your heart and lean not on your own understanding; in all your ways acknowledge him, and he will make your paths straight." (PROVERBS 3:5–6 NIV)

"You will seek me and find me when you seek me with all your heart." (JEREMIAH 29:13 NIV)

"And we know that in all things God works for the good of those who love him, who have been called according to his purpose." (ROMANS 8:28 NIV)

"It is you who light my lamp; the Lord, my God, lights up my darkness." (PSALM 18:28 NRSV)

"[T]hose who seek the Lord lack no good thing." (PSALM 34:10B NIV)

"Praise the Lord! Happy are those who fear the Lord. They are not afraid of evil tidings; their hearts are firm, secure in the Lord. Their hearts are steady, they will not be afraid." (PSALM 112:1A, 7–8A NRSV)

"My soul is weary with sorrow; strengthen me according to your word." (PSALM 119:28 NIV)

"Whether you turn to the right or to the left, your ears will hear a voice behind you, saying, 'This is the way; walk in it.'" (ISAIAH 30:21 NIV)

"Do not rejoice over me, O my enemy; when I fall, I shall rise; when I sit in darkness, the Lord will be a light to me." (MICAH 7:8 NIV)

"If you have faith the size of a mustard seed, you will say to this mountain, 'move from here to there,' and it will move; and nothing will be impossible for you." (MATTHEW 17:20 NRSV)

"The God of peace will soon crush Satan under your feet." (ROMANS 16:20 NIV)

"And God is able to make all grace abound to you, so that in all things at all times, having all that you need, you will abound in every good work." (2 CORINTHIANS 9:8 NIV 1984)

"I have been crucified with Christ and I no longer live, but Christ lives in me. The life I live in the body, I live by faith in the Son of God, who loved me and gave himself for me." (GALATIANS 2:20 NIV)

SCRIPTURE REGARDING FEAR

"The Lord is my light and my salvation; whom shall I fear? The Lord is the stronghold of my life; of whom shall I be afraid? . . . Though an army encamp against me, my heart shall not fear; though war arise against me, yet I will be confident." (PSALM 27:1, 3 ESV)

"I sought the Lord, and he answered me and delivered me from all my fears." (PSALM 34:4 ESV)

"Fear of man will prove to be a snare, but whoever trusts in the Lord is kept safe." (PROVERBS 29:25 NIV)

"So do not fear, for I am with you; do not be dismayed, for I am your God. I will strengthen you and help you; I will uphold you with my righteous right hand." (ISAIAH 41:10 NIV)

"...[Y]our father knows what you need before you ask him ....So do not worry, saying 'What shall we eat?' or 'What shall we wear?' For the pagans run after all these things, and your heavenly Father knows that you need them. But seek first his kingdom and his righteousness, and all these things will be given to you as well. Therefore do not worry about tomorrow, for tomorrow will worry about itself. Each day has enough trouble of its own." (MATTHEW 6:8B, 31–34 NIV)

"For God did not give us a spirit of cowardice, but a spirit of power, of love and of self-discipline." (2 TIMOTHY 1:7 NRSV)

"Do not be afraid. Stand firm and you will see the deliverance the Lord will bring you today. The Lord will fight for you; you need only to be still." (EXODUS 14:13A, 14 NIV)

"Be strong and bold; have no fear or dread of them, because it is the Lord your God who goes before you. He will be with you; he will not fail you or forsake you. Do not fear or be dismayed." (DEUTERONOMY 31:6, 8 NRSV)

"Do not grieve, for the joy of the Lord is your strength." (NEHEMIAH 8:10B NIV)

"Where can I go from your Spirit? Where can I flee from your presence? If I rise on the wings of the dawn, if I settle on the far side of the sea, even there your hand will guide me, your right hand will hold me fast. Search me, O God, and know my heart; test me and know my anxious thoughts. See if there is any offensive way in me, and lead me in the way everlasting." (PSALM 139:7, 9–10, 23–24 NIV)

"When you lie down, you will not be afraid; when you lie down, your sleep will be sweet." (PROVERBS 3:24 NIV)

"Say to those with fearful hearts, 'Be strong, do not fear; your God will come, he will come with vengeance; with divine retribution he will come to save you.'" (ISAIAH 35:4–5 NIV)

"Do not be afraid, little flock, for it is your Father's good pleasure to give you the kingdom." (LUKE 12:32 NRSV)

SCRIPTURE REGARDING GRACE, LOVE, AND TRUST

"The Lord will fulfill his purpose for me; your steadfast love, O Lord, endures forever. Do not forsake the work of your hands." (PSALM 138:8 ESV)

"Surely God is my salvation; I will trust and not be afraid. The Lord, the Lord himself, is my strength and my song; he has become my salvation. With joy you will draw water from the wells of salvation." (ISAIAH 12:2–3 NIV)

"Those of steadfast mind you keep in peace—in peace because they trust in you. Trust in the Lord forever, for in the Lord

God you have an everlasting rock." (ISAIAH 26:3–4 NRSV)

"There is no fear in love. But perfect love drives out fear, because fear has to do with punishment. The one who fears is not made perfect in love. We love because he first loved us." (1 JOHN 4:18–19 NIV)

"Trust in the Lord with all your heart and do not lean on your own understanding; in all your ways acknowledge him, and he will make your paths straight." (PROVERBS 3:5–6 ESV)

"Do not fear, for I have redeemed you; I have called you by name, you are mine. When you pass through the waters, I will be with you; and through the rivers, they shall not overwhelm you; when you walk through fire you shall not be burned, and the flame shall not consume you. For I am the Lord your God, the Holy One of Israel, your Savior." (ISAIAH 43:1B–3A NRSV)

"I have loved you with an everlasting love; I have drawn you with loving-kindness." (JEREMIAH 31:3 NASB)

"'My grace is sufficient for you, for my power is made perfect in weakness.'" (2 CORINTHIANS 12:9 ESV)

SCRIPTURE REGARDING GRATITUDE

"Praise the Lord, O my soul, and forget not all his benefits— who forgives all your sins and heals all your diseases, who redeems your life from the pit and crowns you with love and compassion, who satisfies your desires with good things so that your youth is renewed like the eagle's." (PSALM 103:2–5 NIV 1984)

"The Lord is near to all who call on him, to all who call on him in truth. He fulfills the desires of those who fear him; he hears their cry and saves them." (PSALM 145:18–19 NIV)

"Ah Lord God! It is you who made the heavens and the earth by your great power and by your outstretched arm! Nothing is too hard for you." (JEREMIAH 32:17 ESV)

"See, I am the Lord, the God of all flesh; is anything too hard for me?" (JEREMIAH 32:27 THE BIBLE IN BASIC ENGLISH BBE)

"Be at rest once more, O my soul, for the Lord has been good to you. For you, O Lord, have delivered my soul from death, my eyes from tears, my feet from stumbling, that I may walk before the Lord in the land of the living." (PSALM 116:7–9 NIV 1984)

"I will not die but live, and will proclaim what the Lord has done. The Lord has chastened me severely, but he has not given me over to death." (PSALM 118:17–18 NIV)

"My comfort in my suffering is this: Your promise preserves my life." (PSALM 119:50 NIV)

"Though I walk in the midst of trouble, you preserve my life. You stretch out your hand against the anger of my foes, with your right hand you save me." (PSALM 138:7 NIV)

"Lord, you establish peace for us; all that we have accomplished you have done for us." (ISAIAH 26:12 NIV)

"As a mother comforts her child, so will I comfort you." (ISAIAH 66:13A NIV)

"Because of the Lord's great love we are not consumed, for his compassions never fail. They are new every morning; great is your faithfulness. I say to myself, 'The Lord is my portion; therefore I will wait for him.' The Lord is good to those whose hope is in him, to the one who seeks him; it is good to wait quietly for the salvation of the Lord." (LAMENTATIONS 3:22–26 NIV)

"'The Lord your God is with you, he is mighty to save. He will take great delight in you, he will quiet you with his love, he will rejoice over you with singing.'" (ZEPHANIAH 3:17 NIV 1984)

"But we have this treasure in clay jars, so that it may be made clear that this extraordinary power belongs to God and does not come from us. We are afflicted in every way, but not crushed;

perplexed, but not driven to despair; persecuted, but not forsaken; struck down, but not destroyed; always carrying in the body the death of Jesus, so that the life of Jesus may also be made visible in our bodies." (2 CORINTHIANS 4:7–10 NRSV)

"Blessed be the God and Father of our Lord Jesus Christ, who has blessed us with every spiritual blessing in the heavenly places." (EPHESIANS 1:3 ESV)

"And let the peace of Christ rule in your hearts." (COLOSSIANS 3:15A ESV)

SCRIPTURE REGARDING HOPE

"God is our refuge and strength, an ever-present help in trouble. Therefore we will not fear, though the earth give way and the mountains fall into the heart of the sea, though its waters roar and foam and the mountains quake with their surging." (PSALM 46:1–3 NIV)

"You who live in the shelter of the Most High, who abide in the shadow of the Almighty, will say to the Lord, 'My refuge and my fortress; my God, in whom I trust.'" (PSALM 91:1–2 NRSV)

"When I called, you answered me; you made me bold and stouthearted." (PSALM 138:3 NIV 1984)

"Do you not know? Have you not heard? The Lord is the everlasting God, the Creator of the ends of the earth. He will not grow tired or weary, and his understanding no one can fathom. He gives strength to the weary and increases the power of the weak. Even youths grow tired and weary, and young men stumble and fall; but those who hope in the Lord will renew their strength. They will soar on wings like eagles; they will run and not grow weary, they will walk and not be faint." (ISAIAH 40:28–31 NIV)

"Come to me, all you who are weary and burdened, and I will give you rest. Take my yoke upon you and learn from me, for I am gentle and humble in heart, and you will find rest for your souls. For my yoke is easy and my burden is light." (MATTHEW 11:28–30 NIV)

"Peace I leave with you; my peace I give you. I do not give to you as the world gives. Do not let your hearts be troubled and do not be afraid." (JOHN 14:27 NIV)

"If God is for us, who can be against us? Who shall separate us from the love of Christ? Shall trouble or hardship or persecution or famine or nakedness or danger or sword? No, in all these things we are more than conquerors through him who loved us. For I am convinced that neither death nor life, neither angels nor demons, neither the present nor the future, nor any powers, neither height nor depth, nor anything else in all creation, will be able to separate us from the love of God that is in Christ Jesus our Lord." (ROMANS 8:31B, 35, 37–39 NIV)

"But the Lord is faithful, and he will strengthen you and protect you from the evil one." (2 THESSALONIANS 3:3 NIV)

"The eternal God is your refuge, and underneath are the everlasting arms." (DEUTERONOMY 33:27 NIV)

"I will lie down and sleep in peace, for you alone, O Lord, make me dwell in safety." (PSALM 4:8 NIV 1984)

"You show me the path of life. In your presence there is fullness of joy; in your right hand are pleasures forevermore." (PSALM 16:11 NRSV)

"My soul finds rest in God alone; my salvation comes from him. He alone is my rock and my salvation; he is my fortress, I will never be shaken." (PSALM 62:1–2 NIV 1984)

"When I said, 'My foot is slipping,' your love, O Lord, supported me. When anxiety was great within me, your consolation brought joy to my soul." (PSALM 94:18–19 NRSV)

"'For I know the plans I have for you,' declares the Lord, 'plans to prosper you and not to harm you, plans to give you hope and a future. Then you will call upon me and come and pray to me, and I will listen to you. You will seek me and find me when you seek me with all your heart. I will be found by you,' declares the Lord, 'and will bring you back from captivity.'" (JEREMIAH 29:11–14A NIV)

SCRIPTURE REGARDING PATIENCE AND OBEDIENCE

"For still the vision awaits its appointed time; it hastens to the end—it will not lie. If it seems slow, wait for it; it will surely come; it will not delay." (HABAKKUK 2:3 ESV)

"Do not be conformed to this world, but be transformed by the renewal of your mind, that by testing you may discern what is the will of God, what is good and acceptable and perfect." (ROMANS 12:2 ESV)

"And let steadfastness have its full effect, that you may be perfect and complete, lacking in nothing." (JAMES 1:4 ESV)

"Brothers, I do not consider that I have made it my own. But one thing I do: forgetting what lies behind and straining forward to what lies ahead." (PHILIPPIANS 3:13 ESV)

"If any of you is lacking in wisdom, ask God, who gives to all generously and ungrudgingly, and it will be given you. But ask in faith, never doubting, for the one who doubts is like a wave of the sea, driven and tossed by the wind." (JAMES 1:5–6 NRSV)

"Cast all your anxiety on him, because he cares for you. Discipline yourselves, keep alert. Like a roaring lion your adversary the devil prowls around, looking for someone to devour. Resist him, steadfast in your faith. . . . And after you have suffered for a little while, the God of all grace, who has called you to his eternal glory in Christ, will himself restore, support, strengthen, and establish you." (1 PETER 5:7–10 NRSV)

"I have set the Lord always before me; because he is at my right hand, I shall not be shaken." (PSALM 16:8 ESV)

"Wait for the Lord; be strong, and let your heart take courage; wait for the Lord!" (PSALM 27:14 ESV)

"Trust in the Lord, and do good; so you will live in the land, and enjoy security. Take delight in the Lord, and he will give you the desires of your heart. Commit your way to the Lord; trust in him, and he will do this: He will make your vindication shine like the light, and the justice of your cause like the noonday. Be still before the Lord, and wait patiently for him; . . ." (PSALM 37:3–7A NRSV)

"Be still, and know that I am God." (PSALM 46:10A ESV)

"But my eyes are fixed on you, O Sovereign Lord; in you I take refuge—do not give me over to death." (PSALM 141:8 NIV)

"Restrain your voice from weeping and your eyes from tears, for your work will be rewarded." (JEREMIAH 31:16 NIV)

"For the Lord will not reject forever. Although he causes grief, he will have compassion according to the abundance of his steadfast love; for he does not willingly afflict or grieve anyone." (LAMENTATIONS 3:31–33 NRSV)

"Abide in me as I abide in you. Just as the branch cannot bear fruit by itself unless it abides in the vine, neither can you unless you abide in me. I am the vine, you are the branches. Those who abide in me and I in them bear much fruit, because apart from me you can do nothing. If you abide in me, and my words abide in you, ask for whatever you wish, and it will be done for you. If you keep my commandments, you will abide in my love, just as I have kept my Father's commandments and abide in his love." (JOHN 15:4–5, 7, 10 NRSV)

"Let us not become weary in doing good, for at the proper time we will reap a harvest if we do not give up." (GALATIANS

6:9 NIV)

"For God did not give us a spirit of timidity, but a spirit of power, of love and of self-discipline." (2 TIMOTHY 1:7 NIV 1984)

SCRIPTURE REGARDING SALVATION

"Hear my cry, O God; listen to my prayer. From the ends of the earth I call to you, I call as my heart grows faint; lead me to the rock that is higher than I. For you have been my refuge, a strong tower against the foe. I long to dwell in your tent forever and take refuge in the shelter of your wings." (PSALM 61:1–4 NIV)

"The name of the Lord is a strong tower; the righteous run into it and are safe." (PROVERBS 18:10 NRSV)

"In repentance and rest is your salvation, in quietness and trust is your strength." (ISAIAH 30:15 NIV)

"For we do not have a high priest who is unable to sympathize with our weaknesses, but we have one who in every respect has been tested as we are, yet without sin. Let us therefore approach the throne of grace with boldness, so that we may receive mercy and find grace to help in time of need." (HEBREWS 4:15–16 NRSV)

"The Lord is my light and my salvation—whom shall I fear? The Lord is the stronghold of my life—of whom shall I be afraid? . . . Though an army besiege me, my heart will not fear; though war break out against me, even then will I be confident. One thing I ask of the Lord, this is what I seek: that I may dwell in the house of the Lord all the days of my life, to gaze upon the beauty of the Lord and to seek him in his temple. For in the day of trouble he will keep me safe in his dwelling; he will hide me in the shelter of his tabernacle and set me high upon a rock." (PSALM 27:1, 3–5 NIV 1984)

"You are my hiding place; you will protect me from trouble and surround me with songs of deliverance." (PSALM 32:7–8 NIV)

"I sought the Lord, and he answered me; he delivered me from all my fears." (PSALM 34:4 NIV)

"The angel of the Lord encamps around those who fear him, and delivers them." (PSALM 34:7 NIV)

"When the righteous cry for help, the Lord hears, and rescues them from all their troubles. The Lord is near to the brokenhearted, and saves the crushed in spirit. Many are the afflictions of the righteous, but the Lord rescues them from them all." (PSALM 34:17–19 NRSV)

"Create in me a clean heart, O God, and put a new and right spirit within me. Do not cast me away from your presence, and do not take your holy spirit from me. Restore to me the joy of your salvation, and sustain in me a willing spirit." (PSALM 51:10–12 NRSV)

"Be thou my strong habitation, whereunto I may continually resort: thou hast given commandment to save me; for thou art my rock and my fortress." (PSALM 71:3 KJV)

"You who live in the shelter of the Most High, who abide in the shadow of the Almighty, will say to the Lord, 'My refuge and my fortress; my God, in whom I trust. . . .' You will not fear the terror of the night, or the arrow that flies by day, or the pestilence that stalks in darkness, or the destruction that wastes at noonday. . . . Because you have made the Lord your refuge, the Most High your dwelling place, no evil shall befall you, no scourge come near your tent. For he will command his angels concerning you to guard you in all your ways. On their hands they will bear you up, so that you will not dash your foot against a stone." (PSALM 91:1–2, 5–6, 9–12 NRSV)

"Those who love me, I will deliver; I will protect those who know my name. When they call to me, I will answer them; I will be with them in trouble, I will rescue them and honor them. With long life I will satisfy them, and show them my salvation." (Psalm 91:14–16 NRSV)

"He heals the brokenhearted, and binds up their wounds." (Psalm 147:3 NIV)

"Lord, my strength and my fortress, my refuge in time of distress, . . ." (Jeremiah 16:19a NIV)

"If the Spirit of him who raised Jesus from the dead dwells in you, he who raised Christ Jesus from the dead will give life to your mortal bodies also through his Spirit that dwells in you." (Romans 8:11 ESV)

"For we were so utterly, unbearably crushed that we despaired of life itself. Indeed, we felt that we had received the sentence of death so that we would rely not on ourselves but on God who raises the dead. He who rescued us from so deadly a peril will continue to rescue us; on him we have set our hope that he will rescue us again." (2 Corinthians 1:8b–10a NRSV)

"So if anyone is in Christ, there is a new creation: everything old has passed away; see, everything has become new!" (2 Corinthians 5:17 NRSV)

"The Lord will rescue me from every evil attack and will bring me safely to his heavenly kingdom. To him be glory for ever and ever." (2 Timothy 4:18 NIV)

SCRIPTURE REGARDING TRIALS

"Why are you cast down, O my soul, and why are you disquieted within me? Hope in God; for I shall again praise him, my help and my God. . . . By day the Lord commands his steadfast love, and at night his song is with me, a prayer to the God of my life." (Psalm 42:5, 8 NRSV)

"Behold, I am the Lord, the God of all flesh; is anything too hard for me?" (JEREMIAH 32:27 ESV)

"'My grace is sufficient for you, for my power is made perfect in weakness.'" (2 CORINTHIANS 12:9 NIV)

"I know what it is to be in need, and I know what it is to have plenty. I have learned the secret of being content in any and every situation . . . . I can do everything through him who gives me strength." (PHILIPPIANS 4:12–13 NIV 1984)

"My presence will go with you, and I will give you rest." (EXODUS 33:14 NIV)

"Be strong and courageous; do not be frightened or dismayed, for the Lord your God is with you wherever you go." (JOSHUA 1:9 NRSV)

"You will forget your misery; you will remember it as waters that have passed away." (JOB 11:16 ESV)

"The Lord is a refuge for the oppressed, a stronghold in times of trouble. Those who know your name will trust in you, for you, Lord, have never forsaken those who seek you." (PSALM 9:9–10 NIV 1984)

"Though you have made me see troubles, many and bitter, you will restore my life again; from the depths of the earth you will again bring me up." (PSALM 71:20 NIV)

"My flesh and my heart may fail, but God is the strength of my heart and my portion forever." (PSALM 73:26 NIV)

"No testing has overtaken you that is not common to everyone. God is faithful, and he will not let you be tested beyond your strength, but with the testing he will also provide the way out so that you may be able to endure it." (1 CORINTHIANS 10:13 NRSV)

SCRIPTURE REGARDING WORRY

"It is the Lord who goes before you. He will be with you; he will not leave you or forsake you. Do not fear or be dismayed." (DEUTERONOMY 31:8 ESV)

"Can any of you by worrying add a single hour to your span of life? If then you are not able to do so small a thing as that, why do you worry about the rest?" (LUKE 12:25–26 NRSV)

"Keep your lives free from the love of money, and be content with what you have; for he has said, 'I will never leave you or forsake you.' So we can say with confidence, 'The Lord is my helper; I will not be afraid. What can anyone do to me?'" (HEBREWS 13:5–6 NRSV)

"By his light I walked through darkness." (JOB 29:3 NIV)

"Unless the Lord builds the house, those who build it labor in vain. Unless the Lord guards the city, the guard keeps watch in vain. It is in vain that you rise up early and go late to rest, eating the bread of anxious toil; for he gives sleep to his beloved." (PSALM 127:1:2 NRSV)

"Where can I go from your Spirit? Where can I flee from your presence? If I rise on the wings of the dawn, if I settle on the far side of the sea, even there your hand will guide me, your right hand will hold me fast. If I say, 'Surely the darkness will hide me and the light become night around me,' even the darkness will not be dark to you; the night will shine like the day, for darkness is as light to you. Search me, O God, and know my heart; test me and know my anxious thoughts. See if there is any offensive way in me, and lead me in the way everlasting." (PSALM 139:7, 9–12, 23–24 NIV)

"Your father knows what you need before you ask him. Therefore I tell you, do not worry about your life, what you will eat or what you will drink, or about your body, what you will wear. Is not life more than food, and the body more than clothing? So do not worry, saying, 'What shall we eat?' or 'What shall we wear?' For the pagans run after all these things, and your heavenly Father knows that you need them. But seek first his kingdom and his righteousness, and all these things will be given to you as well. Therefore do not worry about tomorrow, for tomorrow will worry about itself. Today's trouble is enough for today." (MATTHEW 6:8B, 25, 31–34 NRSV)

"Are not five sparrows sold for two pennies? Yet not one of them is forgotten in God's sight. But even the hairs of your head are all counted. Do not be afraid; you are of more value than many sparrows." (LUKE 12:6–7 NRSV)

"Do not worry about anything, but in everything by prayer and supplication with thanksgiving let your requests be made known to God. And the peace of God, which surpasses all understanding, will guard your hearts and your minds in Christ Jesus. Finally, beloved, whatever is true, whatever is honorable, whatever is pleasing, whatever is commendable, if there is any excellence and if there is anything worthy of praise, think about these things." (PHILIPPIANS 4:6–8 NRSV)

"Set your minds on things that are above, not on things that are on earth. For you have died, and your life is hidden with Christ in God. When Christ who is your life is revealed, then you also will be revealed with him in glory." (COLOSSIANS 3:2–4 ESV)

"Cast all your anxiety on him, because he cares for you. Discipline yourselves, keep alert. Like a roaring lion your adversary the devil prowls around, looking for someone to devour. Resist him, steadfast in your faith, for you know that your brothers and sisters in all the world are undergoing the same kinds of suffering. And after you have suffered for a little while, the God of all grace, who has called you to his eternal glory in Christ, will himself restore, support, strengthen, and establish you." (1 PETER 5:7–10 NRSV)

Notes

1 http://www.unmarried.org/statistics/.

2 MJ Blake, *Shutting God Out*, April 5, 2014, http://www.amazon.com/Shutting-God-Out-intimately-purposely-ebook/dp/B00JI0Y0SG/ref=tmm_kin_title_0?_encoding=UT-F8&qid=&sr=.

3 Notes from Pastor Kehinde Adegbolahan: the Assistant General Overseer (Missions) of MFM Worldwide at the March 2012 meeting.

4 Section below paraphrased from Lynn Ponton MD, "What is Forgiveness?" PsychCentral, http://psychcentral.com/lib/what-is-forgiveness/000965.

5 Lynn Ponton, "What is Forgiveness?" PsychCentral, http://psychcentral.com/lib/what-is-forgiveness/000965.

6 Margie Warrell, "How You Can Outsmart Your Brain In Work, Love & Life," July 15, 2011, http://www.forbes.com/sites/womensmedia/2011/07/15/how-you-can-outsmart-your-brain-in-work-love-life/#25c4aa737200.

7 Jack Canfield and Victor Mark Hansen, *Life Lessons for Loving the Way You Live: 7 Essential Ingredients for Finding Balance and Serenity,* April 9, 2013, http://www.amazon.com/Life-Lessons-Loving-Way-Live-ebook/dp/B012YER4SU/ref=s-r_1_1?s=books&ie=UTF8&qid=1458754335&sr=1-1&key-words=9781453275283.

8 Jennifer Read Hawthorne, "Change Your Thoughts, Change Your World," JenniferHawthorne.com, http://www.jenniferhaw-thorne.com/articles/change_your_thoughts.html.

9 Tips 1–4 from "15 Ways to Beat Loneliness," Reader's Digest Best Health, June 2010, http://www.besthealthmag.ca/best-you/mental-health/5-ways-to-beat-loneliness/. Author's notes added.

10 Tips 5–10 from Brock Hansen, "10 More Ideas to Help With Loneliness," PsychCentral, http://psychcentral.com/blog/archives/2012/07/16/10-more-ideas-to-help-with-loneliness/. Author's notes added.

11 John Stibbs, "Emotional Boundaries in Relationships," Hidden Hurt, www.hiddenhurt.co.uk/emotional_boundaries.html.

12 "Why Healthy Boundaries are Important in Relationships," *Kellevision* (blog), December 2, 2009, http://www.kellevision.com/kellevision/2009/12/boundaries-schmoundares.html. Section paraphrased.

13 "A Checklist on Boundaries in a Relationship," The Center for Human Potential, http://www.yourpotential.net/3/5/A_Checklist_on_Boundaries_in_a_Relationship.html.

14 "Why Guys Test Your Boundaries in Dating," Find the Right Man for You.com, http://www.dating-tips-that-coach-women.com/boundaries-in-dating.html.

15 "Basic Introduction to Soul Ties," Great Bible Study.com, http://www.greatbiblestudy.com/soulties.php. Paraphrased.

16 Jotina Buck, "Stop Those Spinning Plates," jotinabuck.com, April 16, 2015, http://www.jotinabuck.com/blog/stop-those-spinning-plates.

17 Ibid.

18 http://christianity.about.com/od/oldtestamentpeople/a/King-Saul.htm.